IS IT THORA?

Also available by the same author:

Happy Days!

Scene & Hird – My Autobiography
(Volume One: 1911 – 1974)

Sing with Praise

Thora Hird's Little Book of Home Truths

Thora Hird's **Praise Be!** *Christmas Book*

Thora Hird's **Praise Be!** *Notebook*

Thora Hird's **Praise Be!** *Prayer Book*

Is It Thora?

Thora Hird

My Autobiography
Volume Two

with Liz Barr

HarperCollins*Publishers*

HarperCollins*Publishers*
77–85 Fulham Palace Road, London W6 8JB

Published in 1996 by HarperCollins*Publishers*

1 3 5 7 9 10 8 6 4 2

A catalogue record for this book
is available from the British Library

ISBN 0 00 627986 4

Printed in Great Britain by
Caledonian International Book Manufacturing Ltd, Glasgow, G64

To my dear and loving daughter Jan
– how clever we were to make a daughter like you.

Contents

Let me explain!

When Thora Hird first appeared on stage in 1911, she did so because the company at the Royalty Theatre, Morecambe, needed a prop doll. In the play a young village maiden is 'done wrong' by the squire's son. Since Thora's mother was playing the village maiden, her father James Hird was the director, and their baby was the requisite few months old, it was handy and convenient for 'our Thora' to be cast in the production as 'the Unfortunate Result'. The Director said to the Actress 'Take *her* on' – and Thora's career was launched.

James Hird was also manager of the Royalty Theatre, and with this job came a house adjoining the backstage portion of the theatre. One part of young Thora's bedroom floor was actually over the backstage wall, and she would lie in bed at night, listening to the actors' dialogue and the audience's response as play after play floated up to her small back room. As she and her older brother, Neville, were growing up the empty stage and property room were their 'playground'.

These were the days of personal advertisements in *The Stage*, frequently including the fact that the person available 'dresses well, on and off'. And the Hirds did.

James Hird had an astrakhan collar to his coat, pale grey spats with pearl buttons and a silver top to his cane, while Mary Jane Hird always wore jewellery bought with savings – because it was easy to pawn. King George V and Queen Mary had just begun their reign, and the Hird family were proud to be members of the 'Theatrical Profession'.

When she was old enough Thora became a member of the repertory company, although, with northern prudence, she kept her day job at the Co-op. Even so, by the time she was 'discovered' by George Formby and signed a film contract with Ealing Film Studios she already had five hundred plays under her belt. She liked to say that she could bring a tray on stage fifty different ways, she'd done *Enter – a maid* so often. With the exception of finding out that on film she couldn't put 'make-up tramlines' all over her face and play characters forty years older than herself, the transition from Morecambe Rep to film parts was a smooth one.

By the late 1940s Thora and her recently de-mobbed husband Jimmy Scott, whom she nicknamed 'Scottie', had moved permanently down to London, selling Prompt Corner, their first small house in Morecambe, and bringing their daughter Janette down with them to the South. It was a big move, but the right one. As a working mother, and by now the main breadwinner of the household, it was agreed that the focus should be on Thora's career, and that Scottie should do the majority of parenting for Jan – a role he fulfilled admirably. Thora gave constant and unqualified love while at home, and sent daily letters, cards and stories by post when on film location or touring in the theatre. Meanwhile Scottie taught, disciplined and generally devoted a large slice of his life to child-rearing.

This arrangement became more and more necessary as a J. Arthur Rank film contract and some successful plays in smaller London theatres were all adding up to establish Thora Hird as one of that famous band of British character actors admired throughout the world, in what had come to be known as 'Show Business'.

Thora's career progressed. She played broad farce with co-stars like Arthur Askey and Freddie Frinton, but also heartbreaking drama in London's West End theatres; Blackpool Summer seasons alternated with Shakespeare on television; roles in films starring Dirk Bogarde, Marlon Brando and Sir Laurence Olivier contrasted with comedies with Norman Wisdom and Will Hay.

And the broadening and developing has gone on. In the last twenty years her association with some of television's leading comedy directors, and with the playwright Alan Bennett, has made her one of television's most respected performers, while her involvement with *Praise Be!* became a cornerstone of the BBC's religious broadcasting. She has also entered the world of books. The first part of her autobiography, *Scene and Hird*, was published in 1976, followed by numerous smaller books full of homespun thoughts of wit and wisdom, many as a spin-off from *Praise Be!* There have also been books especially commissioned for organisations such as Saga and Help the Aged.

During this astonishing career, and helped continuously by her husband and personal manager Scottie,

Thora glided apparently effortlessly from one medium to the next in a world that had changed beyond all recognition from the one her parents knew. Thora adapted her acting techniques to fit the multi-media world now calling itself the 'Entertainment Industry'.

As the years galloped by, there was one subject that Thora and Scottie never mentioned if it could be avoided, the possible death of one of them. They were such a great team, and worked so well together in their private as well as their public life, that it was impossible to think about one continuing without the other. Thora had been suffering from arthritis for many years, having both hips replaced three times since 1980, and more recently having a heart by-pass, so it was tacitly assumed that she would 'go first' and Scottie would retire to the country, to be close to their daughter Jan. Planning for future retirement for herself has never been on the cards for Thora. Her career was their 'family business', and one does not 'shut up shop' and go away while loyal customers still want what you have to offer.

On 30 October, 1994, Scottie died. He was eighty-eight years old. Thora was about to enter the most difficult period of her life.

As with the majority of women of her generation, Thora had lived in her family home until her wedding day. That day she moved out of her father's house and away from his strong – one might say domineering – influence, into the home and under the influence of Jimmy Scott. I don't think it would need a psychologist to see the similarities between the two men, both strong-willed with a stubborn streak, both loving but leaving no doubt as to who was boss, and both unwilling or unable to give words of praise. Thora had spent her entire life trying to please and impress first her father, then her husband. Now, suddenly, aged eighty-three, she was living alone and had no one to whom she could turn to seek approval, no anchor. Her most loving helper and strongest critic was gone.

Even though an incredible closeness had been maintained throughout the years with her daughter, it was Scottie who had always organised her life for her, read all scripts with her, listened to her words ... no major (or even minor) decision had been made without consulting him. He was her cog and wheels. He had seen to all their business affairs – 'did the books', as Thora called it. He had also cooked and shopped, driven her to rehearsals, helped her to dress when arthritis stiffened her joints, and even put her earrings in for her when her own fingers wouldn't work first thing in the morning. He had been the most nurturing of men, and had done these things to allow her the freedom to do what she did best: being 'Thora Hird' – actress, entertainer, raconteur and communicator.

Unlike most widows, the place Thora felt most on firm ground now was not at home, but back at work. So at eighty-four she continues to work and copes with her loneliness in this way. She is happiest on a stage or in a television studio and, most importantly, giving and getting love from the public, who have always recognised her as one of their own.

If there is a secret to Thora's success it is surely this, that every family has a mother, grandmother, sister, cousin or auntie who reminds them of Thora. Yet behind the very loving and human woman, with ordinary weaknesses and frailties, is an extraordinary woman with a giant wit and a formidable artistic and creative talent. In this book she is doing what is closest to her heart – sharing her life with those she loves.

'And so, Ladies and Gentlemen, it's Showtime! Turn on the spot-light. Roll cameras. It is an honour, a pleasure and a privilege for me to present to you the star of our show, your favourite and mine, the one, the only, Dame Thora Hird!'
   – Good luck, Mum!

Janette Scott Rademaekers
February 1996

Introduction

I don't know of many people who are asked to write their autobiography ... *twice!* We only live once, so when I wrote my autobiography *Scene and Hird* when I was sixty-five (published in 1976), I thought that that would be that. I had written it mainly for my grand-children, Daisy and James, who were still very young then, and living in America. I wanted them to have something so that when they grew up they would be able to read it and learn about me ... from *me*.

But nearly twenty years have gone by since then – in a flash. And how many people do you know who have had the busiest, most productive time of their lives ... between the ages of sixty-five and eighty-five? But think of this: when the last volume was published I was still to meet and work with Alan Bennett; I was still to begin seventeen years of presenting *Praise Be!*; still to do *Hallelujah!*, *In Loving Memory*, *Flesh and Blood*, *Last of the Summer Wine* ... and – well, as much work, if not more, than I'd done in the preceding twenty years. So many lovable, comical, interesting things have happened since I wrote *Scene and Hird*, and still keep on happening ... you'll think I'm being immodest if I tell you how many publishers have asked me to write another volume ... but they have ... so I have. First of all, let me explain the title, *Is it Thora?*:

When you appear regularly on television you become what is called 'a household name'. A nicer way of saying that is that people think of you as part of their family. I was already 'a household name' in the 1970s when I wrote *Scene and Hird,* because as well as my films and theatre work I'd made appearances in television series such as *Dixon of Dock Green* and *Z Cars,* and starred in two long-lasting and – I'm thankful to say – very popular television series, *Meet the Wife* and *First Lady.* When I was doing *Meet the Wife* so many people thought my co-star, Freddie Frinton, really was my husband, that if they saw me out with my real husband – Scottie – they'd say things like 'Never mind, Thora! You deserve your fun! We won't tell Fred!'

But if ever I thought I was 'a household name' before, it was as nothing to what was to happen after 1977, once I started presenting on BBC, on Sunday evenings, the popular hymn request programme *Praise Be!* One of the main things that happened was that everywhere I went strangers would greet me – not because they recognised me as someone from television, but really as though they knew me – as if I were an old friend or a member of their family. And this is where 'Is it ... *Thora?*' comes in.

Whenever Scottie and I had any shopping to do in Oxford Street, which was pretty often, we nearly always went early in the morning to be there when the shops opened – half past nine, ten o'clock. One day, after I'd been doing *Praise Be!* for a few years, we were going into Marks and Spencers for something. The doors had just opened as we got there and there was a smattering of people inside. We walked in, and coming towards us was quite a tall, rather genteel lady, with her daughter. Now this lady was what, in a repertory company, you'd cast as 'the Vicar's Wife'. I mean that very flatteringly – vicars' wives don't all look like that, but that's what you would have cast her as, in a play.

She came out with something that always makes me laugh: 'Oh! Is it ... *Thora*?' Not 'Are you Thora?' They always say 'Is it Thora?' I've had that said to me so often ... and I bet you never thought I was going to finish the explanation I started pages ago, did you?

Well, on this day I had said yes, it was ... *I* was, and – really to my surprise – she burst out crying. And just for a second I felt a bit embarrassed so I said to her, 'Oh dear! I'm not that ugly, am I?' And she looked at me and said, 'No! It's because we love you such a lot!'

Then she started to tell me that her daughter, who was with her – that's when I found out that it was her daughter – had had four miscarriages and was pregnant again. I said, 'Well I'm sure this time God will let the baby be born. I'll be putting her in my prayers tonight.'

Now this lady had got both her arms stretched out to hold me just underneath my shoulders, if you can just visualise the position, rather like a bridge. And at a counter near us – for vests – there was a little lady, no more than four feet nine, very blonde hair cut quite short – I'm sure that if she could have had a cigarette in Marks and Spencers, she would have had one in her mouth. Anyhow, there's the Vicar's Wife, the tall lady, hands just underneath my shoulders, looking at me and talking earnestly, and Little Thing at the vests counter turns round, sees what's going on, rushes over, ducks under the Vicar's Wife's arms, puts her little face up under my chin and says 'Who's bluddy luvely ...? *You* are!' And went! Disappeared! But what I think is so funny is that the lady, the Vicar's Wife, never even noticed anybody had popped up underneath. Anyhow, I said how nice it had been to meet her, and Scottie and I went out of Marks. We never even got what we'd gone there for – and I'm a shareholder!

We got back into Oxford Street, crossed the road and were going down on the other side of the road, when we heard somebody running. Now just because I hear somebody running, I'm not conceited enough to think they are running after me, but there was somebody pelting along behind us at such a pitch, and when they arrived it was a little man about as tall as the lady from the vests counter, and he looked up at Scottie and said, 'Can I kiss 'er?' Scottie didn't have time to say 'With pleasure!' or 'Do you mind?' before the fellow bobs up, kisses me on my chin, and then continues running down Oxford Street ... Scottie looked at me and sighed, 'Shall we go home, love?' I said, 'I think we'd better! I think we've had our Cabaret for today!'

There's another reason I've called it *Is It Thora?*, I mean apart from it being something people say that makes me laugh. It is because I do sometimes wonder to myself, when I sit and think about all the things that have happened to me – *is* it Thora? People seem to see me differently, somehow, from how I see myself.

Introduction

Have all these things, like getting the OBE and being made a Dame, really happened to the little girl from Cheapside, Morecambe who used to scrub her mother's steps ... and didn't know what the word 'arse' meant?

Well, I try to live up to it, and what helps me most is all the love I get from people. In the first part of my autobiography I wrote a lot about Cheapside, where I spent my very happy childhood with my loving, wonderful mother, father and brother, and although *Is It Thora?* is a continuation from where I left off in 1977, I've included some more stories about the old days too. So many things that happen to me in the present seem funnier or stranger because of the way things were in the past, so I'm not likely ever to forget.

I'm grateful for all the love that I have been blessed with all my life. I sometimes think that I've had more than my fair share of love. No woman could have had a more loving husband than Scottie, or loved their husband more, during the fifty-eight years of marriage we were blessed with. I honestly believe that it is *because* I loved him so much, and still do love him, that I've been able to keep going and keep cheerful since October 1994, when he died. I have so many wonderfully happy memories, and writing this book has helped to bring them all back to me.

Anyway, here goes. *Is* it Thora?

Yes – it – is!

1

On the strait and narrow

I didn't write anything much about my religion in the first part of my autobiography. It wasn't that I wasn't religious then – as I've said many times when being interviewed, there was never a moment in my life when I could say 'Oh, I've found God!' because God has always been *there*, part of my life.

I've always talked to God – sometimes I think I'm inclined to ask him to help me a bit too much. I always seem to be saying 'It's me again ...' In a television studio there's always a floor manager, who is the contact between the artist or artists in the studio, and the producer and director upstairs in the control room, which is called the Gallery. I am convinced that I ask for so many things from God that sometimes he says to his floor manager 'Who is it?' and if the reply comes 'It's Thora' he sometimes has to say 'Oh, tell her I'm out!'

I've always had my own picture of Jesus. I've often spoken about having four uncles who were all Morecambe fishermen, but I must get that in again because Morecambe shrimps are the best in the world. (Her Majesty the Queen has Morecambe shrimps.)

My Uncle Robert had what I've got – in those days it wasn't called arthritis like now. It *was* arthritis like now, but you didn't call it that. You called it rheuma-tism. Anyhow, my Uncle Robert had had to stop trawling because he couldn't move about. One day he was sitting in our kitchen, his hands on his stick, and even now, eighty years later, I can see those hands, with the bones twisted. All my uncles had beards and black hair like retriever dogs, all curls. (Why are men given curly hair? My brother had all the curls, while I have the straightest hair in the world – *in the world*, not just England.)

Our house was always one for 'Rat-a-tat-tat ... Are you there, Mrs Hird?' And it was usually to borrow something. I say that with great love. Vinegar, two candles, a cupful of sugar, or my favourite one: 'Mrs Hird, my mother says have you got a piece of brown paper and some string, because she wants to send a parcel.' I can see my mother, folding up the brown paper whenever it came round a parcel.

(I do that myself. Not out of any meanness – if it's a lovely sheet of brown paper I could no more put it in the bin than I could put myself in the bin. I fold it up. I've also got a box in the kitchen painted red with 'string' on it, for all the little bits of string.)

However, there's my uncle Robert sitting, hands on his stick, and there's a rat-a-tat-tat and a neighbour comes in, because our door was always open. 'Oh, Mrs Hird, my mother says could you lend her an egg-cupful of vinegar?' Then she says 'Hallo' to my uncle, because everybody knew everybody in Morecambe, and when my mother gives her the egg-cup of vinegar she thanks her and is about to go out – and you don't wonder that in some of the parts I play I remember these ladies, because the things they did quite naturally were more comic than anything anyone could do who was trying to be funny – and she says 'Ee, Robert, tha does look like Jesus!'

I was five. I looked at him and I thought, 'He does! He looks like Jesus. He looks like the little tracts they give us at Sunday School.' But from then on I always pictured Jesus wearing a blue 'ganzie' – our name for the blue Guernsey sweater that fishermen wear, with buttons up one side of the neck – and with a cap over his thick black curls.

When I got to about ten I had a serious phase. I was saying my prayers one night, and I'd been wondering for a while if Jesus really *did* look like my Uncle Robert, when I had another thought – that he *didn't* look like my Uncle Robert, and I shouldn't *think* that he looked like him. It was wicked. My mother, as always, was sitting on the bed, and I was kneeling beside it, and I looked up and said, 'Jesus doesn't really look like Uncle Robert, does he?' My mother took my face in her hands, kissed me on the forehead and said, 'Who says he doesn't?'

And now, aged eighty-four, because I had such a wonderful, understanding mother, I still sometimes think that Jesus looks like my Uncle Robert!

I must admit, religion isn't an easy subject to write about in an autobiography. You can't very well put 'I am very religious ...' But I'd like to say something about it, because, of course, since I wrote the first part, as well as continuing with my acting career I have done seventeen years of presenting – with great love and pleasure – a religious programme on the BBC, *Praise Be!*

All the time I was presenting *Praise Be!* I would get people 'telling me off' in the street! I could go down one of the main streets in London and some lovely old lady – I say 'old lady', how dare I? I'm an old lady myself! – would stop me. I don't mean rudely, just *slightly* aggressively, and she would say, 'Hey! You never played that hymn I asked for! I sent for that hymn because my sister Connie loved it. And you never played it ... you never read her name out.' Then I had all the explanation of 'Well you see, we had sacks of requests, and I'm very sorry ...' As often as not, it would turn out that I *had* played her favourite hymn, and that what she was upset about was that I hadn't read out her sister Connie's name. Anyway, we would always finish up friends, but I might get ten yards further on and somebody would say, 'Oh Thora! D'you mind if I just requested a hymn?'

When I first started presenting the programme, in 1977, we were in 'Green', one of the studios at the BBC Television Centre, big enough for an audience of 350 if we'd wanted one, and in this huge space there was just a chair, a monitor (that's like a television set) and me. I must say, I looked very lonely sitting there on a little platform on my own.

They would put the hymns we were playing on the monitor, because, as some of you know, the hymns were all taken from *Songs of Praise* – in fact, for the first couple of years my series was called *Your Songs of Praise Choice* – but that was a bit of a mouthful, and I'm glad they changed it. I would watch each hymn being sung on my monitor, and then I would turn to one of the three cameras that was bearing down on me, to do what was known as 'Thora's Link'.

In about the fourth programme a hymn on the monitor was being sung by a choir of little boys. There they were, aged about six or seven, little pale blue jumpers on, little pale blue ties, and they were singing 'All things bright and beautiful', and it was lovely. And all of a sudden one little fair-haired lad in the middle of the front row turned to his friend to smile, and all down the side of his face was a birth mark, I think you call it a 'strawberry mark'. And I don't know ... it just upset me so much. The hymn finished and I was cued in to say the next link, but I couldn't because I was crying. The producer and director and the technicians were all upstairs in the Gallery – and I said, 'Someone in the Gallery could have warned me about that!'

The floor manager came over and said, 'They are very sorry. They didn't mean you to be upset.' I said, 'Well, in the future, if ever there's anything like that and I have to speak immediately after it, will you warn me in some way?' So they had to play the hymn through again, and cue me again, and this time I was all right.

About three programmes later there was another row of children, only this time they were all either on crutches or in wheelchairs, all brave, all smiling and singing beautifully. Before they came on the floor manager came over to me and said, 'The director says I have to tell you it's "One of Those".'

In those days I used to wear semi-evening dress, with a rose in my cleavage. I don't know, it seemed a different programme then, a bit more formal. One man wrote and said, 'I've noticed, Thora, that at the end of every programme you say "God bless ... I'll be

5

back next Sunday." But how do you know you'll be back next Sunday? You should say "God willing (or DV – Deo Volente), I'll be back next Sunday."' Another one wrote to say 'I love your programmes and I've watched every one. I love the hymns, I love the way you do it, I love the way you dress, I love the way you speak ... but I don't like your pink nail varnish!'

I took all these checks very lovingly. I never wore pink nail varnish again on that programme, and I always remembered to say 'I'll be back next Sunday *– DV!'*

We moved to a smaller studio for the next couple of years, into what is known as the Presentation Studios, where they do things like the weather. In those days Barry Took was presenting *Points of View* in Presentation Studio A while I was doing *Your Songs of Praise Choice* in Presentation Studio B. (And may I interject at this point that I was one of many thousands of viewers and fellow-artists who were all very upset when Barry was unceremoniously removed from presenting *Points of View*, which he used to do so brilliantly.) Many's the time Barry and I have sat side by side, sharing the minute dressing room, having our noses powdered together!

The smaller studio made it more homely, and we began to have more homely sets, too, with lamps and plants and a comfortable sofa, making it look as though I was doing the programme from my own living room, and I'm sure that that's what many viewers thought it was. A year or two after that, and for many years to come, we really did make the programmes from my home – or rather my daughter Jan's home – but I'll come to that in another chapter.

From the very first series the viewers' letters arrived in sacks. Bill Cotton Junior was then in charge at the BBC, and Dr Colin Morris, a Methodist like myself, was head of religious programmes, and when they were asked how long they thought *Praise Be!* would last they said, 'Until Thora falls off the edge of the pier!'

It changed my life in some ways. For one thing, I've so many friends now who wear dog-collars. And they are all great chaps, I can tell you. Roger Royle, who was doing *Songs of Praise* and *Good Morning Sunday* on Radio 2 for most of the time I was doing *Praise Be!*, often pops in for a cup of tea and a chat; John Tudor, Rob Marshall, Rob Garrod, Colin Morris ... all my friends, and all dog-collars! And I've met as many Bishops as any actress could ever hope for!

I see Colin Morris every year at Wesley's Chapel in the City of London, where we are both invited for their annual 'Carolthon'. I remember one year, standing in the very pulpit John Wesley himself used to preach from, and I noticed from the Order of Service that after I'd stopped speaking the next carol would be 'While Shepherds Watched'. The organist sits just underneath the great pulpit, so I leaned over and said, 'Is that to the usual tune?' and he nodded, and I said, 'Oh, I wish one year we could sing it to Lyngham! It really goes so well to that. That's the tune the Salvation Army Band always used to play when they came down Cheapside on Christmas morning, when I was a child.'

Anyway, we sang it to the normal tune that time, but the following year they invited me again, and I noticed that once again the carol following my little bit was 'While Shepherds Watched', so when I came to the end I leaned over and asked the organist 'What tune?' and he smiled and said, 'Lyngham!' and I said, 'Oh, thank you! That's the best Christmas present you could have given me.' And Paul Hulme, the minister, said, 'We've gone one better than that, Thora. Look up in the gallery.' And I looked, and a Salvation Army Band were standing up in the gallery above me! They'd come along especially for me, to play Lyngham.

So you see, for me, religion isn't just about keeping on the 'strait and narrow' – it's much more about kind hearts, laughter, and loving, joyous moments like that.

2

In Loving Memory

In April 1978 Ronnie Baxter, the director, and Dick Sharples, the writer, came to London to give me the script of a new series, called *In Loving Memory*. They wanted me to play Ivy Unsworth, the wife of Unsworth the Undertaker, played by Freddie Jones. In the first episode Unsworth dies and Ivy becomes the undertaker herself, with the help of her hapless nephew, Billy, brilliantly played by Chris Beeney.

I said to them, 'Well, I won't read it while you're here' – because I never do that – 'but will you tell me, before I read it, is there the slightest chance that I could ever hurt anybody that had been bereaved?' To which Dick Sharples said, 'Do you think we would have brought it to you if there was?'

I suppose I enjoyed doing *In Loving Memory* as much as any series I've ever done. Ronnie Baxter is a great director, one of the best comedy directors in the business, and Dick Sharples is a very clever writer. Chris Beeney was a pleasure and a joy to work with, Avis Bunnage, God rest her soul – what a good actress, and what a good friend – played the next-door neighbour, Joan Sims was in it for several episodes, another very professional, excellent actress who always makes me laugh, and a lot of other very big names would be in it for a day.

And we didn't hurt anybody. At the read-through on the first day of rehearsing an episode, if there was ever the slightest likelihood that there was anything that might pain anybody, then out it would come. I can recall one occasion there was a quotation from the Bible. With *In Loving Memory*, eight times out of ten it opened with me on the telephone. I'd put on my 'posh' voice and say 'Unsworth's the Undertakers ...' – until I knew it was only a neighbour or someone who knew me, when I'd change to speaking normally. This time it began with someone ringing up to ask for a stone, and I had to get out the book of suitable quotations for putting on headstones – 'Rest in Peace' and things like that. The words that Dick had written for me to suggest for this headstone were from the Bible: 'The Lord giveth – the Lord taketh away ... Blessed be the name of the Lord.'

Now, in the early days of the BBC you couldn't say 'My God!', you had to say 'My goodness.' In fact there was a green book of things you couldn't say and do. A lot of jokes are made about it now, things like how if an actor was doing a scene when he was in bed with an actress, he always had to keep one foot touching the floor.

But it wasn't because of the green book that I didn't want to say this line of Dick's. I didn't want to say a quotation from the Bible, or the Prayer Book, to make it sound like a funny line – in fact I definitely wasn't going to. I am experienced enough to know it would be bound to offend somebody somewhere.

I said at the read-through 'We can't say this – it's from the Bible' but just for once Dick did not agree with me. I admire Dick Sharples immensely, and will enjoy acting his words as long as I live, but on this occasion he wasn't very pleased. He said, 'Well it won't matter!' I said, 'Well, it will matter to me.' He said, 'You mean you're not going to say it?' I said, 'No Dick, I'm not ... this will hurt somebody.'

I was adamant, and in the end Dick said, 'Well, I'll write you something else, but it won't be *"comic"* enough for you.' He was really mad. He used to go downstairs to write any new bits. He came back up into the rehearsal room about a quarter of an hour later and skimmed a piece of paper across the table at me, saying 'There you are. See if you can make anything of that.'

He hadn't rewritten the whole scene, just the words I was supposedly reading out of Ivy's book of suitable engravings for headstones. Instead of the Bible quotation, he had written: 'Ta-ra, Grand-dad! All the best. The North lost a good'un when you went west!' Brilliant! I said to Ronnie, 'They'll be able to do a row of knitting during this laugh.' Which was right. By heavens, when we were doing it in front of a live audience, the howl of laughter we got on that line.

Comedy isn't just about learning the words. Well, of course you all know that. You know that this thing called 'timing' is important, which means getting the rhythm of comedy, getting a laugh just by the way you hang a coat on a nail, having the courage to pause just that split second longer than the audience can bear, until everyone is on the edge of their seats with wondering what you are going to say ... and then coming out with it.

There's another thing in comedy. When you have a

comic reply to something somebody has said, if there is a word too many the music of it goes. What I mean is, comedy questions and answers are really music. And one morning in *In Loving Memory* I thought, 'I'm not going to get as big a laugh on this line as I could do if there was a word less.'

I'll put it in 'ta-ra-ras' in this book, so please read it as I put it. If someone says to you 'Ta-ra-ra-ra-ra-ra-ra-*ra*' you've got to, in comedy, answer 'Ta-ra-ra-ra-ra-ra-ra-*ra*' to get the laugh. Do you see? With real words, I mean. But if there is a word too many and you have to answer 'Ta-ra-ra-ra-ra-ra-ra-*ra*-ra' it doesn't work. It sounds silly, but this is really very important in comedy.

One morning I happened to say to Ronnie Baxter, 'I shan't get the laugh I'm hoping to on this, because there's a word too many – the music is wrong.' And he hugged me and said, 'I didn't think anybody ever said that but me!'

Ronnie and I had such an understanding about comedy. Brilliant man, he was, a brilliant man. He's not directing any more; what a loss to television.

Sometimes real life is funnier than fiction. I remember a letter from a girl who wrote 'This really happened. My uncle George died last week, and for years he has told my auntie "I want cremating" and my auntie has always said to him "No, no. You're going to be buried."' – Well, of course it's very difficult, when you're dead, to stick up for what you want. Anyway, this girl said she and her auntie were travelling along in the funeral cortège, and suddenly out of the back of the hearse she saw smoke, and she said to her auntie,

'There's smoke coming out of the hearse!' and eventually the hearse stopped, and they pulled up behind it, just outside Marks and Spencers, in the high street. The driver of the hearse came and said, 'We're going to have to leave you here just for ten minutes, because we're going to get another hearse.' They took the coffin out and put it on the pavement, guarded by two of the bearers who were going to carry it when they got to church.

People were coming in and out of Marks and Spencers, practically having to step over the coffin, while she and her auntie waited in the car. Two ladies came out and one said to the other, 'Well fancy leaving a coffin outside on the pavement like that!' and the other one said, 'Oh, it's Thora, look, it'll be Thora's show, *In Loving Memory*, because there she is in that car!' It wasn't me at all, it was 'auntie'! The girl wrote that she was sure that the smoke was a message from her uncle to her auntie, saying 'I want cremating, remember!'

Such a lot of funny things happened when I was doing *In Loving Memory*, but I think the thing I remember most was the Great Train Journey of 1979. I went up to Leeds from King's Cross every Thursday at lunchtime – I've done that journey so many times over the past twenty years – camera rehearsal on Thursday night, put it into the can on Friday, in front of an audience of about 350, and an early train back on the Saturday morning to be back in London by half past ten or eleven o'clock and have the rest of the day to spend with Scottie at home.

One week, during the winter when we had the very

heavy snows, Avis Bunnage, Joan Sims and I all got on the 12.25 train together, from King's Cross to Leeds. I've always loved Joan Sims. She really does make me laugh. We would often travel back together as well, on the breakfast train the morning after a recording. They'd put the breakfast in front of you, and in those days – I don't know if they do now, because you've got to be very wealthy to afford a breakfast on the train these days – but then there was bacon, egg, sausage, tomato, black pudding, fried potato and a piece of fried bread. And as soon as they'd put it in front of us, before we'd even picked up our knives and forks, Joan would say 'Are you going to eat that sausage?'

But on this occasion we were going up *to* Leeds. Avis was sitting opposite me, next to the window on the corridor, and Joan was next to her. Next to me was a man from an oil rig, his shirt open down to his navel. We're cold, we're freezing, but he isn't. He takes a packet of cigarettes out and pushes them at me and says, 'Do you want a fag, flower?' In one corner is a lady who's going to Leeds to set up a stall with perfumes and wonderful beauty creams at an exhibition. She never gets there, I'll tell you now. In the other corner is a man with a very expensive briefcase, who has got to be at a meeting at half past seven. He won't get there either, I'll tell you for nothing. The corridor is full of businessmen, all standing and pressing against the door. So you've got the picture.

The train sets off and we've been going about twenty minutes when Joan says, 'Er ... Have you brought any sandwiches, Avis?' And Avis says rather sharply 'Yes!' with clearly no intention of opening them *yet* – because there wasn't always a buffet on the train. Meanwhile the train is travelling slower and slower because of all the snow on the line ...

Eventually we get to Doncaster, and out we spew, only to find that five trains before us had done the same thing – there was not an inch on that platform. Joan steps off the train into snow so deep it goes over the top of her boots. We manage to fight our way into the waiting room and find seats while we wait for the next train to take us on to Leeds.

Now, we are due to do a camera rehearsal that afternoon, for a show that we are going to record the following day, and it's a bit important that we let them know that we're not going to be there – because we're not, the way things are looking.

Avis Bunnage was a very able person – I think she must have been a Leader in the Guides – and she knows that, to find someone who works on the railway you have to look for someone with a uniform on that doesn't fit them. So Avis sees a man wearing a coat with sleeves hanging down over his fingertips, and he even has a clipboard and pen, so she says, 'Excuse me, could I trouble you for a moment?' and makes him follow her into the waiting room, where we all are. Avis is very business-like and polite. She says to him, 'I want you to ring up Leeds television studios. This is the number.' He says, 'Oh yes?' She makes him write down the number on his clipboard, and then says, 'Ask for Floor Four.' By which time, he's hypnotised is this man. 'Floor Four?'

'Yes, and then ask for Mr Baxter. Mr Ronnie Baxter. Have you got that down? Let me look. Yes, that's the number. That's the floor. Now, what you say to Mr Baxter is ...' At which point he says,

15

'Here! Hold on a minute, missis ...'

'Listen! This is very important. Tell Mr Baxter we are marooned on Doncaster Station – as you can see we are – and it is possible that we won't be there in time for the camera rehearsal. What are you going to say?'

And like a child at school, he says, 'Tell Mr Baxter you're marooned on Doncaster Station, and you can't get there for the – what rehearsal?'

'Camera rehearsal.'

Strange to say, I have to tell you now, he did exactly that!

However, we're still sitting there. We've eaten the beetroot and tongue sandwiches. Joan's had two of the eggs, and Avis and I have shared the other egg. Avis goes to her bag, to put the pen back that she'd got out for the man, although he didn't need it, and a Mars bar shows itself. 'Oo! There's a Mars bar there!' says Joan. So, Avis cuts it in three with her nail file, and we have a third each.

Eventually a train comes in. Well, of course, there is not a hope of getting on it, with all these people. We wait a bit longer. Another train comes in. Not a hope. We finally get on the third one, and the man from the oil rig gets on with us. He says it is taking him longer to get from London to Leeds than it had taken him to come from Kuwait, or wherever it was he was working on the oil rig. Meanwhile Avis has found a cellophane bag of mints in her bag and, seeing a lot of businessmen who look as though they haven't eaten for a year, she goes along the coach, saying 'Would you care for a mint?' and everybody takes one. (I'm telling you all this so you'll understand what very glamorous lives we actresses do lead!)

We got to Leeds after nine, very worried that they would have missed us. They hadn't really. Ronnie and Dick came into my room at the hotel and told us that they'd received our telephone message and had had a very good camera rehearsal without us – Ronnie Baxter had played me, Dick Sharples had played Avis and I forget who had played Joan.

Then the three of us had to go down for dinner, because Joan was nearly dying of hunger.

In Loving Memory ran for many years, but people always remember the first one, where the coffin fell out of the hearse, careered down the hill, turned the corner, and shot into the canal. They always remember that. And how we had to throw the wreaths down from the bridge, like a sea burial.

As I say, we had to be so careful about hurting people with a comedy about funerals, but I had many appreciative letters from people who had just lost someone, saying that the series had cheered and consoled them. Because we weren't making fun of bereavement – what we were making a little gentle fun of was pretentiousness, and the way that so many of us, let's face it, know very little about religious rituals. And yet we all have to undergo this very serious ceremony when saying goodbye to our much loved friends and relations. And because it so often happens when we are trying to be at our most solemn and dignified, all dressed up in our best clothes, that something very comical happens ... and we want to laugh, and we *know* the person we are saying goodbye

17

to would have laughed, but because of the solemnity of the occasion, we feel we mustn't.

I always hoped that *In Loving Memory* might help people to stop worrying or feeling guilty about having wanted to laugh at the funeral of somebody dear – by showing them that laughter and loving memories go very well together.

3

Praise Be!

During the seventeen years I was presenting *Praise Be!*, for many people, especially lonely people, I think I almost became like one of the family. So many of the letters started in almost exactly the same way:

Dear Thora,
I hope you don't mind my calling you Thora, but I feel
I know you. It's like having a friend coming into my
living room for a chat on a Sunday evening when you
are presenting the hymns on Praise Be! ...

You cannot know what pleasure those letters gave me. But some of them were very sad, and many of them really made me weep.

I recall a letter from Northern Ireland. It said,

Dear Thora Hird, I have a little boy who is
maladjusted. He is ten years old. He has never really
spoken, but when you come on the screen in Praise
Be! *he puts his hand out and says "Thora!" Please*
don't answer this letter, because I am the only
Protestant in this street.

A letter from another lady said,

19

*My husband doesn't really know what's on television,
but he watches it because it occupies him. But when
you come on, I can tell by his face ...*

Well, then it makes it worth while being an artist, or
being whatever I am. I used to laugh sometimes, when
people would write to say 'I don't know what it's
called, the hymn, but this is a line in it ...' Well, there
are a lot of hymns in a lot of hymn books to look
through to find a line!

I could fill a book with the things that happened to
me when I was doing *Praise Be!* – and come to think of
it, I have written several books about it already! I
always enjoy telling the story of one day when I was
making *In Loving Memory*. We had a shot that was
quite long – if I said to anybody in our business 'It was
four pages of script', they'd say 'Well, that's a pretty
long shot'. We had just over eighty extras for this shot,
because the scene was the funeral of Billy, my nephew,
who wasn't dead really, of course, because it was a
comedy, but I thought he was dead ... So his best
friend, Ernie, was driving the hearse, and Ronnie
Baxter, who is such a splendid comedy director, went
round to every one of the extras saying things like
'You take your handkerchief out and wipe your eyes.
Sir, will you please raise your hat as the cortège
passes. You, lady in maroon – just break into tears ...'
And he really gave them each an acting part to do.

Right, so it's a long take. Eighty extras all standing
ready. Ronnie Baxter has set up a camera some
distance away to get a picture of the whole scene. We
wait for the light to come just right – a golden evening
light that you get over these pretty Yorkshire towns

that are on steep hills. The very end of the shot was of me getting out of the car behind the hearse, and saying 'Ernie! What d'you think you're doing?' because he'd stopped the hearse.

As I got out of the car to say my line a lady in a red trouser suit, cigarette in the middle of her mouth, walked into our scene from the side of the road, where she'd been sitting on a wall watching. She came right up to me and said, ''Ere! you never played that 'ymn I asked yer to play, and it was my favourite, and it was me mother's favourite!'

I said, 'I'm very sorry'. The cameras all stopped rolling the moment they saw her. I said, 'But you see, it's very ...' and I got so far, and Ronnie Baxter came up and said, 'Excuse me, Madam! We are filming.'

'*Are* yer?' she said. 'Where? Why? Where is there anything?' meaning cameras. He pointed to where they were and said, really very politely, 'And if you wouldn't mind just clearing the shot, you can speak to Thora when we've done it.' So off she goes, back on the wall, and we have to do it all again, from the top, the women blowing their noses, the men raising their hats and all the rest of it. I get down out of the car and say 'Ernie! What do you think you're doing?'

'Cut' says Ronnie, and *immediately* on comes the red trouser suit again. Another cigarette. 'No, I mean, it's like I said – you never played that 'ymn that I sent for, and you see it was me mother's favourite ...'

I said, 'Well, er, I'm awfully sorry, Madam, I wish I could please everybody, and I do try to. As a matter of fact the hymns are chosen usually by the most requests there are for them. So in that way we do please most people.'

She said, 'Well it wasn't mine you played.'

'No, well I'm very sorry. Which hymn was it?'

And she looked at me, with the cigarette stuck right in the middle of her mouth and she hesitated – 'The, er ... With, er ... Well! I can't remember which 'ymn it was *now*. But it was me mother's favourite and you never played it!'

One Saturday morning I went with my sister-in-law, Rita, to the market at Crowborough, where they have a regular car-boot sale. Rita, Scottie's sister, is a retired Headmistress, so we're all very proud of her. I always call her Miss Brain of Britain. She is a kind, loving auntie to Jan, and after she retired she came to live not far away in Sussex, which meant a lot to Scottie, who was always very close to her.

The first stall we looked at was full of wonderful old postcards, the kind of postcards that you bought when I was a kid – all new, they were not written on or anything – so I bought some of those, then strolled along looking at bits of things. On one stall there was a little jug, bronze coloured, and it really was nice. I picked it up and I said to Rita, 'Isn't this nice? Couldn't you see that full of marigolds?'

I said to the man, who looked like a farmer, with his big red face and rolled-up sleeves, 'Excuse me, how much is this, please?' He said, 'Is it for you, Thora? Have it for nothing.' I laughed and said, 'Well, you're not going to retire very quickly at that rate, giving all your stuff away!' But he said, 'No. I'd like you to have it. My wife ... thought there was nobody like you.' And he burst into tears. It's heartbreaking, to see a man cry. It is really very upsetting. I said to him, 'Oh dear. What's the matter?' And he said, 'She died last week.' And I could see this man fighting his grief, this big farmer, with his shirt sleeves rolled up, standing there ... I said to him, 'Is the pain like a brick in your chest?' And he said, 'Yes. Yes. I'll never get over it.' And I said, 'I know what it is. God gives you that brick. He gives one to everyone who has loved someone very much. And you carry it round in your chest, and it hurts so much, but only because you loved them so much. And God will take all the points off that brick gradually – not that you will love your wife any less ... but this he does. He takes the pain away. He's not going to let you grieve for ever.'

He blew his nose, and I said, 'One day you'll wake up and think, "Eh, that brick's gone." You won't notice it going, but it really does go.'

I have always treasured that little jug, which he insisted I accept as a gift. A few weeks later I was presenting *Praise Be!* from Jan's house in the country, and I was reading out someone's name who had requested a hymn, and as I did so – I was in the kitchen and to the right of me I noticed the little bronze jug, full of bluebells – it looked like a painting. I said, 'Oh, just a minute, doesn't this look nice?' The camera took a shot of the flowers in the jug, and I told everyone the story of the farmer who had given it to me, and when I'd finished even the camera crew were moved. And afterwards I got so many letters from viewers saying 'That's it, Thora. It is just like a brick.'

You can't really put a price on moments like that, and so many happened during the seventeen years I was presenting *Praise Be!* It isn't that *Praise Be!* made me more religious, but it made me more aware of religion. The letters came in *sacks*, and you've no idea what was in some of those letters – the stories of troubles and loneliness and worry. They altered me as a person.

I'd receive letters from many an old lady, seventy-something, eighty-something, saying 'I lost my husband two years ago. Life is very lonely without him ... Sometimes your face on television is the only friendly face I see all week ...' Do you wonder they often made me cry? I can remember one time I was reading the letters after Jimmy had gone to bed, and as usual some of them were bringing on the tears. And he came in, in his pyjamas, and he said, 'Are you coming to be ... What are you doing? Oh! I'll tell you, darling, if you are going to upset yourself like this, I'm going to have to ask you to stop doing the programme.' And when he said that, I thought, 'Oh no. I couldn't stop doing the programme.'

Of course I did eventually. But it taught me a great deal, *Praise Be!*, about the troubles people have, the thousands of lonely people there are, and the great faith so many people have to help them bear and overcome their sorrows. And it's made me realise, more than ever, how very lucky I am.

4

I'm not Beryl

I grew quite used, on *Praise Be!*, to receiving letters to 'Dear Flora', 'Dear Dora', and 'Dear Nora'. I didn't mind too much being confused with Dame Flora Robson, Dora Bryan or – I suppose – Nora Batty! My name is rather unusual, because it comes from a mournful Victorian ballad my mother used to sing called 'Speak to me, Thora!' sung over someone's grave!

Scottie and I, when we had an afternoon free, were very fond of getting on a boat at Westminster Bridge and sailing as far as Greenwich. It was a lovely sail, and I especially liked the man who did the patter, when he said '... and on the left is *Cleera-patra's* Needle.' He always pronounced it like that – and we used to enjoy it so much on a sunny afternoon.

One day we had some friends over from Stockport, Bill and Anne Price, very dear friends of ours. We'd been out to lunch in town and it was a beautiful day, so we decided to take them on the river trip to Greenwich.

Well, there are several shops when you land, and as we passed one shop there were several of those dolls that laugh. I don't know how to describe them if you haven't seen them – there's just this 'ha-ha-ha!' going on. I thought, 'Now that would be a bit of fun, to buy one of those and put it in the toilet.' Because the one I saw rather looked like a box you would press for some perfume to spray over you. But if you pressed this one, all you'd get was 'Ha! ha! ha!' So all four of us went in the shop and we were looking round, and there were jokes and all sorts of things. A very well-dressed lady came in, looked gratified to see me, came over smiling and said 'Hallo ... Beryl.'

And I thought, now I must be careful, so I said 'Hallo' because it seemed the polite thing to do.

'Now when are you going to be on television again?'

I said, 'I think perhaps you think that I'm Beryl Reid?' and she said very challengingly 'Yes!' So I said, 'Well, I'm awfully sorry, I'm not Beryl Reid.' And she said very firmly, *'YOU ARE!'* so I said, 'Well, do forgive me, but I do know who I am – and I'm not Beryl Reid.'

She said, 'You are – and I'll tell you something else – the public are your living. It's your place to be polite to people who watch you on television.'

'Well, I'm quite sure you're right. But I can't pretend to be Miss Reid when I'm not. I do know her very well, and I'm fond of her, so do please excuse me.'

And with that she huffed herself out of the shop, talking to herself, quite convinced that I really was Beryl Reid pretending not to be. And that was that. So we bought the little thing for the loo – and on the pavement is the same lady, with three friends. And they whisper something, and she marches up to me – I can't say she strolls up to me – and says, 'You are *NOT*

Beryl Reid.' So I said, 'No. I know I'm not. I told you I wasn't.'

'You didn't!'

'I did. You said "Hallo Beryl" and I said, "I think you think I'm Beryl Reid and I'm not"...'

'Well just you remember – the public are ...'

'Yes, thank you, I know. The public are my living. And I try not to be rude, and I hope I'm not being rude now, and I'm very sorry I'm not Beryl.'

'Well, remember that. You are *not* Beryl Reid!' and she walked off.

So I'm just telling any of you who are reading this, in case there's any confusion in your minds – this book is *not* by Beryl Reid, and it's not by Nora, Dora or Flora – it's Thora!

5

Meet the family

Families are such precious things. Even now, in my prayers at night I always say to God, 'Thank you for my mother and father and brother, and thank you for the way they wrapped me in love until I was old enough to meet Scottie, who wrapped me in another sort of love.'

On 3 May, 1987, Scottie and I celebrated our fiftieth wedding anniversary. I knew there was a lot of skul-duggery going on that we weren't supposed to know about, but we did know that Jan and her husband William were arranging a luncheon for us. The first surprise was that it was on a barge, on the Regent's Canal. They secretly invited people we had known and loved for ever, and there were speeches and lovely food and lots of laughter as we sailed round the Regent's Canal on a beautiful morning and afternoon. It really was marvellous.

But that was only the first part of the surprise. Jan had told us to pack our bags, and bring our passports, and that she and William would be going with us. I had honestly no idea where we were going, and when we got to the airport we still didn't know where we were going. But the man driving the little motor car that took us to the Departure Lounge said to me, 'Do you like Sicily, Miss Hird?' and I said, 'Yes – is that where I'm going?' So that's when we knew. (I *had* been wondering why we needed our passports for a journey round the Regent's Canal!)

Jan was born on 14 December. And, if I may digress for a minute, something that was very different in those days was how you were treated after childbirth. I mean, today, if you'd had your baby on 14 December you'd be up and about finishing your Christmas shopping, dusting the house and so on by 15 December, wouldn't you? But in those days mothers had a long period of 'lying in', when they weren't supposed to do anything at all and just stayed put in bed for two weeks, with the District Nurse calling round every day to make sure you did so. I remember the Christmas Eve, ten days after Jan had been born, all the family were round and they'd all looked in on me and Jan upstairs in the bedroom, wished us Happy Christmas, cooed over her ... and then they had gone downstairs. I could hear them all talking and laughing and having a good time, and I got a bit fed up of being on my own upstairs, so I picked Jan up out of her cot and started to walk down the stairs with her to give them a surprise ... Well! Consternation! Even Scottie – who was the mildest man you could ever meet – shouted at me, 'What do you think you are doing with that baby!?' You really would have thought they had caught me trying to murder her!

What can I say about Jan? Words can't describe how I feel about her. She's been the most loving daughter any parents could wish for, and a tower of strength to me since Scottie died. She gave up filming when her children were born to become a full-time mother, and that's another role she has played to perfection. And I have to say, she still looks like the cover of *Vogue* when she comes out with me for a lunch or something. But you'd expect me to be proud of my own daughter, wouldn't you? So I won't embarrass her any more.

Every parent would like to give their child everything. But they can't, because if they could I would have given Jan the long, happy marriage I have had. On the other hand, if the choice has been unfortunate in a marriage and they haven't found the right one, I'm afraid that I agree very much with them parting. When you discover you've married the wrong one, the misfortune is *there* – in the choice. There's no point in saying it hasn't happened. If there are children they are bound to suffer one way or another. This happened to Jan, but thank the Lord she's very happily married now, to William, and has found all the love and happiness she deserves.

I must give credit where credit's due to our son-in-law, William. He and my Scottie were so close, they became like father and son. He's like Scottie in some ways.

William makes the bread at their house, and it's scrumptious. Every breakfast-time you can partake of William's brown or white new crusty bread. He mixes the flour and stuff the night before, and it mixes and bakes during the night, and hey presto! it's all there and ready for breakfast. (Any of you who owns one of those fantastic Japanese bread-making machines will know how it's done.) Anyway, it's scrumtially-doodillus. Can you just imagine it, with a large cup of beautiful coffee?

Jan has given us two wonderful grandchildren, James and Daisy. I'm so proud of them. My father, my father-in-law and my husband were all called James. And now there's my grandson, James the fourth, six foot one, a handsome lad who looks like Scottie, so there can't be much wrong with that. He's at UCLA (University of California at Los Angeles) at the moment, having been educated in England, at Cumnor House and then at Lancing.

Everybody says Daisy is extremely like me (poor little soul!). Daisy was at Cumnor House and then she went to Benenden. (And if it was good enough for Princess Anne, I reckon it was good enough for my grand-daughter.) Daisy is following in the family tradition of going into the acting and entertainment business. I'm not quite sure about James. We'll have to wait until after he graduates. I must admit, when I saw him play Mozart in *Amadeus* at his school, he was so good ... that I couldn't tell him. This is true. It's a part that shrieks to be overplayed, and he never did. I was very proud of him, but later, when I met him with some of his friends, I couldn't tell him how good he was. I thought they might think, 'Oh, well, it's just his grandmother.' So I wrote to him the next day, and I think he's still got the letter.

When Daisy was a little girl, living in America, on one of my twenty-three visits and Scottie's twenty-six visits – we were always nipping over – Scottie made an egg custard. Now in our part of the country an egg custard is a deep, beautiful pastry crust, and then the egg custard poured in, a little bit of cinnamon on the top, and baked in the oven. It goes to just about the consistency of a blancmange. Ooh, writing about it I could just eat some now!

However, it was the first time Daisy – a little thing, two or three years old – had had one, and her Poppa, Scottie, said 'Eat up your egg custard, Daisy' but she wasn't quite sure about it, and I came in and, really to encourage her, like you do with small children, I said, 'Ooooh! Egg custard!' And all day we had her coming up and saying, 'Ooooh! Egg custard!'

The thing is, it has gone on all through life. I know this sounds rather silly, but we never write to each other without a mention. I usually try to do a little four-line poem about it, but the difficulty is that not a lot of words rhyme with it. There's mustard, flustered and clustered. But not many. In fact I wrote to her the other day, and ended with a little verse – but I had to use flustered again. I put:

> *So as you read these loving words*
> *I beg you don't get flustered*
> *It's just a letter – nothing else ...*
> *I wish it was egg custard!*

It's a lot of nonsense, isn't it? But we do this, and she 'egg custards' me, on the telephone. We'll have a long conversation from America and she won't have said it, and I'll be saying goodbye and saying, 'I love you so much, darling' and she'll say, 'And I love you, Ganny ... Ooh, ooh! And egg custard!'

Daisy plays the piano and sings beautifully – she and James are both musical. They get that from their father, Mel Tormé, but also from Scottie. Daisy has a job in sports promotion, which she took on the understanding that she can have time off for auditions. It's the heartbreaking time, that makes you or breaks you, going along for part after part. I remember it so well, and feel for her so much. I think she'll finish up as an actress. She really is comic, but not in the sort of music hall way that I am.

To be honest, I very rarely see myself in her, but I'll tell you when I do see myself, and that is when she'll be over here in England and it will come the day to fly back, and she will come round to say goodbye, and say in a very small, wobbly voice, 'We're not going to cry ... (sniff) ... are we ...?' And the car will be waiting to take her, and I'll be sobbing and I'll say, 'Don't be like that – it's like me.' And I don't want to be like that either, because I don't want Jan seeing it. Jan has been extremely brave in her life. Her children come and go. They must be as well travelled as anyone of their age.

On 17 January, 1994, Daisy rang Jan from Los Angeles and told her there had been a terrible earthquake half an hour earlier, but that she was all right and that although all the lines were down she was ringing from her car telephone, which was working. It was the early hours of the morning over there, our lunchtime. Daisy told Jan her television had flown through the air and the walls of her condominium (flat) had cracked from side to side, so she was driving to Coldwater Canyon (where her father has a large house built on rock, which would be safer). She had an old school friend from Benenden, Julie, staying with her, and she was all right too.

Jan telephoned from Chichester and reported all this to us, so Jan in Sussex and Scottie and I in London sat anxiously waiting all that day for the next call from America. All day the television was reporting that all the telephone lines were down, the San Diego Freeway, one of LA's main highways, had collapsed, and explosions and floods and mud slides were taking place across Los Angeles, which was in complete darkness.

After about an hour Jan telephoned us again to say that Daisy and Julie had, after a dreadful journey, arrived safely in Coldwater Canyon. Because all the power lines were down and there was no electricity at the house, Daisy had faced her car onto the front and left the headlights on, to light up the inside of the house. Good old Daisy!

We were still worrying about James, who we hadn't yet heard from, until Jan rang to say that she'd heard that he had also managed to reach the Coldwater Canyon house safe and sound. Thank God.

I feel for Jan so much when the children go back to America, but, as she says, it is the best country for them to be in if they really want to make successful careers for themselves in the entertainment business. There's so much more going on there. But I remember how much I hated it during the fifteen years Jan was living in Beverly Hills. When I knew she was unhappy I wrote to her almost every day, even if it was just a note scribbled on the back of a script during a break in rehearsals, to tell her how much we loved her. I see I've written entries in my diaries 'Sent letter number ? to Jan.'

And I know she's the same with her children. Aren't we daft?

6

Listen with Thora

When Daisy was a little girl I'd make up stories for her. Sometimes I'd write them in letters and sometimes I'd tell them to her, whenever we visited them all in Beverly Hills. I remember once I'd bought her a pair of little party shoes in Kensington High Street. I saw them in the window and they were so pretty, in silver brocade with a little golden strap, I couldn't resist them. We were going to America the following week so I took them with me.

I was about to give them to her and then I thought, no, we could have a bit of fun with them. We were all sitting near the bathing pool one morning and I was telling her a story about a little girl who met a fairy, making it up as I went along, and Daisy was sitting there, looking up at me, listening so solemnly with her chin on her hand, and as I got to the end I said, 'So you see, although she hadn't got what all the other little boys and girls had, the fairy said, "We'll give her a little surprise all of her own, something beautiful and fairy-like ... I know, let's hide it in the garden, where she'll find it." And that night the little girl went to sleep, knowing that the following day she was going to hunt all over the garden to find her fairy surprise.'

Daisy said, 'And does the little girl find the surprise

the next day?' And I said, 'Oh! Certainly. Because the fairies promised it!' After she'd gone into the house for her lunch, there I was, scooting round the garden looking for somewhere to hide these shoes. There was an apple tree with a lot of foliage at the bottom, and flowers, so I hid the box among the flowers. After lunch, when Daisy came out again she said, 'So – if the surprise is still there ... could I find it?' And I said, 'Oh, I do hope it *is* there, and I do hope you *do* find it!'

Well, I was so excited, but do you know we were there from two o'clock until nearly twenty to five! She went here, she went there, she looked and she looked, but she never went anywhere near where I had hidden the box. I was beginning to think I'd have to tell her where it was, because I was getting a bit fed up of this by now. I said, 'Oh, Daisy! There was a bit of the story I didn't tell you. There were some beautiful apples near where the fairies lived, and the fairy said to the little girl, "Would you like an apple?" and the little girl said, "Oh, thank you! I would love an apple." The fairy went to the apple tree to fetch her an apple, and as she tried to get it, it fell, because she was only a little fairy. Oh dear me! So the little girl bent down to find the apple, which had fallen down and got hidden among a lot of beautiful flowers. And what do you think she saw? ...'

And she was off! She disappeared – whoosh! In a minute she came back with her parcel, all done up with ribbon. And it was her little face, when she opened up this box and found the silver shoes the fairies had left her. It was worth anything.

I love all children's books and stories. There's never any malice in them. I like to think that one day I might write some children's stories myself. I've read quite a lot of stories for children on radio and television – I love doing it. I was very flattered to be one of the first people to be asked to read the Paddington Bear stories on television, and afterwards Michael Bond gave me a signed copy of the book. I have it at home now, with the yellow pages of script stuck inside it, because on television you have to read a shortened version of the stories. I probably shouldn't be telling you this, but you do, because you have to fit the words to the pictures.

Anyway, I loved reading about Paddington Bear, and of course I always love reading stories for Jackanory. Years ago now I read all the Mrs Pepperpot stories. I think she was my favourite. She had a little striped skirt on, red hair in a little red bun – I used to think she looked a bit like me. Delightful stories. But on one occasion, I remember, we had a few technical hitches, and the producer, Jeremy Swan, had to keep interrupting me. Things went like this:

THORA: 'Hello! I'm going to read to you about Mrs Pepperpot. Now you remember Mrs Pepperpot, don't you? ...'

JEREMY: No ... (hold on!) ... you what? (Sorry, Thor! Just a minute, love) ... Right. Yes. (Sorry – not you, darling.) Right! OK. Cue Thora.

THORA: 'Hallo! I'm going to read to you about Mrs Pepperpot. Now you remember Mrs Pepperpot, don't you? ...'

JEREMY: No! (Sorry, Thor!) Well are you right now?
Yes. Good. Yes. Right. (Yes, it's nothing
you're doing, Thor! Just some ...) Right.
Good. OK. Cue Thora.

THORA: 'Hallo! I'm going to read to you about Mrs
Pepperpot. Now you remember Mrs
Pepperpot, don't you? ...'

JEREMY: NO! (So sorry, Thora. There's a gremlin
somewhere) ... Right? OK. Cue Thora.

THORA: 'Hallo! I'm going to read to you about Mrs
Pepperpot. Now you remember Mrs
Pepperpot, don't you? ... *Don't* you? Oh
well! Sodyer if you don't remember her,
because I'm not going to sit here, reading
this, if you don't remember her!'

Quite some time later, I was in my dressing room at
the Manchester studios, where we were recording
Flesh and Blood and there was a knock on the door, and
there he stood, armful of flowers, and as I opened my
mouth to say, 'Hallo, Jeremy!' he was saying, 'Do you
remember Mrs Pepperpot? *Don't* you? Well sodyer, if
you don't remember her!'

To this day he's never forgotten it!

I was blessed with very good parents. My father –
who, by no means could you call a 'religious' man, but
I know that he believed in God – he read the Bible
fourteen times from front to back. Not fifteen, not thir-
teen, fourteen – and I know, because he told me this so
often. He would say to me, 'Read it. Read it often, and
understand it. It's the best book you'll ever read.'

After a pilgrimage you see the Bible differently. The

stories come to life. The distances between places are much smaller than I'd ever imagined, and everything becomes so real and vivid.

I was asked recently to read twelve stories from the Old Testament, on cassettes for children. These Bible stories are so interesting when they are told *as stories*. Even in the days when I was doing *Praise Be!*, when I would sometimes be asked to read from the Bible, I tried never to sound like a female vicar. The Bible really is full of wonderful tales of men and women and their adventures, and if you read it as an actress, and not in a special 'churchy' voice, you get more out of it. Well I think so. Reading these Old Testament stories for children this time, when I had just come back from a pilgrimage to the Holy Land, well, I could hardly describe it as a job of work, I enjoyed doing it so much. Later on I did twelve more, from the New Testament. And by the time this book comes out I will have had the joy of recording the whole of *The Life and Death of Jesus* on cassette.

It's when I'm asked to jobs like that that I sit for a bit sometimes and think to myself, 'Are you really good enough for this?'

7

The Olde Lofte

Our home in London is in a Mews and we've lived there ever since Scottie was demobbed after the war.

You have to come in under an archway by a pub and walk down to the bottom of the Mews to find us, walking across cobbles. When we first arrived the cobbling was beautiful, because in the old days they were artistic with the cobbles, every one had to be the same shape. It came up in the centre, like the sun coming up, so the rain could run down the cobbles. And some people still kept hens on the side.

Some time ago now they re-did it, and it's never been the same since. They don't look like anything now. For every five cobbles they took out, they put three back, and instead of packing soil between them, like before, they put concrete. I suppose they made quite a good job of it, but it's never been the same, and they are always having bits up for electricity and such. It took them so long to re-do it, there was one little man who almost became a relative, we saw him so often. We asked him to stay one evening to concrete under our stairs, where we keep the wine, because before that it was just earth. Every morning, going out to rehearsals it would be, 'Good morning, Thora!' all the way up the Mews.

The cobbles in our garage are Staffordshire Blues. If you bought one now it would cost the earth – well, you couldn't get 'em now, anyway. I wouldn't know Staffordshire blue from Coventry pink, but Jimmy knew, because he had spent many years in Staffordshire.

We've given some very good parties in the Mews, especially on New Year's Eves. We've had up to seventy people in the garage – you couldn't get seventy people upstairs in the flat, but the garage could hold five cars – if you packed them like dominoes. We had laid half of it with a wooden floor when we first moved in, because Jan was learning to tap-dance with Jack Billings – a lot of professionals will remember Jack Billings – and we used that as a dance floor, for the parties.

We tried to keep everything as it was. The four horse stalls are still there, although the wooden partitions dividing them have long gone. The Staffordshire blue cobbles still cover the floor. If you look up you can see the squares where the food chutes were, where the hay and oats came down for the horses. There's also a chute where you can put a little lid down, the front has a handle so you can stop it when you've had enough. And if you lift the carpet up in our flat up above, you can see the same squares, only, of course, they've been boarded up now.

In the old tack room at the back of the garage are all the heavy iron hooks for the horse collars, bridles and the rest of the horse trappings. There's a tiny iron fireplace so the coachman or driver could keep warm while he cleaned the harness and horse brasses, and there's an iron sneck (Lancashire for handle) on the door.

41

Most people have the tack room taken out to make more room in their garage, but we kept ours. I've always loved all these old things. Jimmy had it as a workroom. His drumkit is still in there – two pea-boilers, side drums, bells, cymbals and everything.

Upstairs, between the lounge and the dining room windows, looking out over the Mews, is a hay-gate. There is a door, and if you open the door there's the wooden gate. It's very attractive. I have plant-pots fastened on it, and flowers in front. I keep the door open all day, and hear people coming and going, up and down the Mews ... life going on. I wouldn't be without that gate. I love it. The first thing I do in the morning is open the door to it.

And a loving thing about it was, when I would be coming home from work and the car that brought me back would stop in front of the house, Scottie would hear me and he'd hang over the hay-gate and call down, 'Don't bother getting your keys out, I'll come down!' And I don't have to say that I miss that very much these days.

We call the whole lot The Olde Lofte. It's full of love and memories. Who would want to leave all that? Not me. It's like me – old but well preserved.

8

Handles

Now in this chapter I'm speaking as a lady of eighty-four. Here's me with my arthritis, my stick and all the rest of it. But when I was a little girl, and we lived next door to the Royalty Theatre in Cheapside, in the foyer of the theatre, outside the Dress Circle doors ... I can see it now as I write this – all that red carpet. There were two lots of double doors, and they each had very large brass handles on them, cleaned by a lady with one eye called Mrs Randall. And if I was being comic I would say, 'I do not remember the name of the other eye!' Mrs Randall polished the handles until they shone like gold; when I was little I thought they *were* gold.

Well, as the years rolled by a very sad time came when the Royalty was going to be demolished – which it never should have been, I don't mind adding. And it was a Bradford firm that were demolishing it: I thought, 'It would be a bloomin' *Yorkshire* firm!' Anyhow, they did get on the telephone to me, and said that they understood that it had been such a big part of my life ... and really, it had, when you think how I started in Rep there; I'd played on the stage and under the stage as a child, because we had lived next door for so many years. Yes, I *loved* the Royalty

Theatre. And I don't think that's a misuse of the word.

Anyhow, they asked me was there anything I would like as a souvenir? I thought immediately, 'Yes, please. I would like a set of the Dress Circle door handles.'

They sent them to me, and they now grace the left-hand side of the staircase in my London house. But you see, I didn't think when I was tripping about blithely at the age of four, thinking they were made of gold, that they were going to assist me to go upstairs when I was eighty-four – which they really do. I've got a banister on the other side of the stairs, but those handles help me, and every day I think about the Royalty – up the stairs, down the stairs. And they still shine.

At the bottom of the stairs I have the Exeter Theatre 'pass door' handle. A 'pass door' in a theatre, for anybody who doesn't know – please don't think I think you don't know, but these are terms that, unless you've worked in the theatre you probably wouldn't know – is usually on the left-hand side of the auditorium, and it passes from the stalls to the stage (have a look next time you're in a theatre), and it is private. You have to have permission to use it. It isn't something anybody can just open and go onto the stage. Well, I have the handle of the Exeter Theatre 'pass door' on the bottom door in the Mews. And on the door going into the garage I have the handles from the St James Theatre, in London. So every handle holds a memory, and they all shine so beautifully I'm afraid of finger-marking them sometimes.

I have mentioned many times in articles and things how fond I am of brass. I don't know why I get to like these things that want cleaning – all my life I seem to have been cleaning something. But they look nice, you see, they look so nice as they shine. I'll tell you something else I've got on my staircase – a set of weights, eight pounds, four pounds, two pounds, one pound, half a pound – shining like solid gold. I bought these when I was doing *First Lady*, the drama series where I played a councillor. We used the Barnsley Council Chamber in the Town Hall. There was a councillor there, a real one, a particularly nice lady who invited me to lunch one day, saying she wanted to show me something. Well, she took me into Wonderland! It was a warehouse, imagine this, *full* of scales, like there used to be in shops, that had a marble thing that you put the bacon on, and all these weights. I thought, 'I'll buy two sets of weights, because they'll remind me of when I worked at the Co-op.'

So now, every time I'm going up or down the stairs in my London house I'm reminded both of the Co-op and of the Royalty Theatre, two wonderfully happy and loving periods of my life.

May I say at this point, I don't profess to be the world's greatest authoress, in fact I'm not so much an authoress as much as a person having a little chat with you all. Not that you get the chance to correct me, or answer me back, but most of you who read my efforts *know* me. Well, I mean you know me well enough to understand what I write about, and how I would say things in a chat with you. So let's say I'm like a friend who has nipped into your home for a little chat, and this being a book – you can 'shut me up' whenever you wish!

If you are reading my efforts in bed, you can put

them down at any time, as I haven't written everything chronologically, so 'Goodnight and God bless' to
any reader who is just about to snuggle down and
drop off!

9

The Mill House, Isfield

Jan met William in America in 1978, at a dinner party in a mutual friend's home. They had both been through broken marriages; William had four children, Jan two. Understandably, neither of them was in a rush to marry again, but as time went by and they saw that all their children mixed in well, they spent a lot of time together and, eventually, in April 1981 they were married in America, in the home of William's best man, the author Barnie Leason.

They married at noon, and then got the six o'clock evening flight back to England, where at long last she was coming home to live. It was joy unbounded for us.

I remember the day, a few months before the wedding, when they came to the Mews and they were so excited, with Polaroid pictures they'd taken of The Mill House, Isfield. It was a lovely old house, big enough for William's four children, who often visited, and Jan's two, to all have a room each. Really, it was a little estate. There were fourteen acres, with a wood and two meadows and a river running into a lake. There were two greenhouses – a big old-fashioned Victorian one that was heated and a modern one with a vine, planted by William, and there was even a dear little cottage, which we eventually moved into ourselves in April 1982, which had originally been a cowshed.

As time went by Scottie and I did the cottage up and furnished it, and we had a conservatory built on the back. We both worked hard on the garden, which really became very pretty, though I say so myself. We had such happy times there, although we couldn't get down there as often as we'd like, because if I was filming or rehearsing early on a Monday morning it was too far to go down there just for two days.

Whenever we were at Isfield I used to love to wake up in the early morning (five-thirty to six o'clock is a magic time) and walk round our garden. As I strolled along, mug of tea in one hand, my faithful stick in the other, the smell of fresh grass, trees, flowers and weeds (and don't forget a weed is only a flower in the wrong place!) permeated the early morning air. The noise of birds getting up – our privet hedges were always packed with nests – was deafening.

The smell of new-mown grass is marvellous in the summer months. Before very long Jan would appear with her dogs, Lucy, Tess and Patch, and they would come up to me and sit looking very pathetic until I reached in the pocket of my duffel coat to give them their first biscuits of the day, four each. Scottie would join us, and those were the magic moments when I was so aware of having *everything* ... everything that matters.

I know a lot of you will be familiar with the Mill House and its beautiful grounds, and the dogs and

48

ducks and geese that lived there, because for many happy years it became the setting for *Praise Be!* Once Jan and Bill had settled in we recorded all the programmes there, and for about ten days each year the BBC would take over the ground floor. They weren't originally supposed to have all that, they were just supposed to be in the living room, but Jan, being such a professional herself, suggested that they use the dining room as a 'producer's gallery' for everyone not needed on 'the set' – i.e. her living room – so they could sit and watch on a monitor, for which they were very grateful. But it didn't end there. Valetta Stallabrass, who was the very good, very dear and loving director of the series for many years, and has become a great family friend, was soon suggesting that we record some of the links by the inglenook fireplace in the study ... and some in the kitchen ... and some in the conservatory. To cut a long story short, by the time the series finished we'd recorded *Praise Be!* links in every downstairs room of the house, and all over the grounds – in the woods, beside the lake, having tea in the rose garden, looking for mallard ducks' nests, gathering daffodils ... you name it, we filmed it. One year, after the director had said, 'Right. That's a wrap!' I said, 'Are you sure? Are you quite sure you don't want to take a shot of me upstairs in the four-poster bed? You've been everywhere else!'

Every year for that week, although the household was disrupted and the hall was full of cables and ground sheets and there was always someone in the downstairs loo, no one minded and we were like one big happy family. For me it was great, because at lunch-time I just had to walk twenty-two steps across to the cottage to have lunch with Scottie, and the make-up girl would come across to help me change and make up for the afternoon show. Or we'd all go out to the local pub, the Laughing Fish. Members of the crew used to put in a special request to the BBC to come back each year, so we usually had the same cameraman and sound man, and even the autocue operator, Jeremy, used to contrive to be back with us every year.

Jan used to arrange the flowers, often having picked them from her own cutting beds, but some were ordered in – and she would often take part in the programmes by doing a reading, or coming in to chat with me on the show, because we got so many requests every year from people who wanted to see her, especially to hear her read, because she does read beautifully. Scottie, Daisy and James, and even William put in appearances over the years, so viewers began to feel they really knew the whole family ... In fact, Daisy can only have been about ten the first year she was on, James two years younger, and as the programme went on for so many years you almost saw them growing up on *Praise Be!*

As for the ducks and the dogs – they were regular scene-stealers. One day we had to pretend I was telling the dogs the story of St Francis of Assisi, and how he loved all God's creatures. The viewers saw me telling the story, and Lucy, Tess and Patch gazing at me in rapt attention, their faces looking for all the world as if they were thinking, 'Oh, St Francis! Oh what a kind man!', the occasional tail thumping. What you couldn't see were three biscuits on the ground in front of them, or Jan, just behind the camera, commanding them to 'Wait! Trust!' As soon as I finished it was 'Good dogs – take!' and three noses plunged forwards to gobble up the biscuits.

The series began one year with me leaning out of the window, and just as I did so a procession of about ten Muscovy ducks waddled by in front of the camera. You couldn't have planned that, or trained them to do it. It was just one of the moments of magic – of which there were many, and I've written about them in my *Praise Be!* books – that all made recording *Praise Be!* at the Mill House such a joyous thing.

The other thing that we all loved about our time at Isfield was our church and our friendship with the wonderful vicar, Roger Dalling, who was like a magician the way he conducted services, and especially the way he told stories to the children, stories which held us all spellbound.

The ancient parish church of Isfield is along a beautifully kept country lane, just opposite the Mill House gates. The river Uck runs close by, and you can still see remains of locks from when it was a busy thoroughfare for barges. You can also see the earthworks of a medieval wooden fortress that guarded a ford in the river. And there was once a Roman road just to the west, running due north all the way from Newhaven to London. So once the little church would have been at the centre of all the main thoroughfares, not hidden away at the end of our little country lane. The great Roman and Victorian empires have grown up – and faded away again – all around that little church. But it's still there, and I'm sure it will be for centuries to come.

10

Hallelujah!

When I was doing the series *Hallelujah!* for Yorkshire television in the early 1980s, written by Dick Sharples, I played Salvation Army Captain Emily Ridley, aged forty-two.

When you are making a programme about something like the Salvation Army, you always take a lot of care not to offend them in any way. Any television company will be careful about that. We had to have a technical adviser from the Salvation Army to let us know whether we were going too far – or not far enough. And I'm happy to tell you, according to the Salvation Army we never went nearly far enough. They said some of the stories they could tell were even funnier than the ones Dick was making up.

That was how I met Rob Garrod of the Salvation Army, who was a captain himself then and their Director of Public Relations – he's something much higher up now. He was our technical adviser and we became good friends, and through him I often became involved with doing things for the Salvation Army proper. Whenever I went to the citadel in Oxford Street to make a personal appearance, on the back wall there would be a big photograph of me, in the uniform and the bonnet, which I was always rather proud of – I quite fancied myself in that bonnet!

I am still invited to many Salvation Army events, including the big 'Carolthon' they hold every year in their citadel in Oxford Street. One year Princess Diana was on the platform as well. Before the show we were all gathered in a room drinking orange juice and cups of tea. It was the first time I'd met her, although I've met her many times since. She's a great giggler, as you probably know, and she was so lovely and natural it was just like talking to ... you! We chatted about one thing or another for a little while, and I was longing to ask her what her favourite hymn was, for *Praise Be!*, but I didn't have the cheek. Then it was time for her to lead us all on to the platform in front of the audience, and as she was going – I don't know whether she'd read my mind, or what – she leaned back and said with one of her giggles, 'By the way, my favourite hymn is "Breathe on me Breath of God" – with the descant.'

When filming out of doors you usually wear a small microphone, concealed somewhere on your person, with leads connecting it to a battery transmitter, which you hide in a pocket or somewhere. The sound assistant will come to clip it on just before 'shooting' starts. For *Hallelujah!* my uniform fitted me like a glove because it had been tailored for me by the Salvation Army's own outfitters, so the transmitter had to be clipped on to the back of my skirt to be hidden from view, and the wires had to come down from the mike, which was pinned on the inside of my blouse, under my skirt, and back up between my legs to connect to the transmitter at the back. Do you follow?

Well, we were filming on an ordinary pavement, just outside Leeds. The mike was already pinned to the inside of my blouse, and the sound assistant came to fix the transmitter to the back of my skirt and connect it up with my mike. Now forgive the way I tell this, because however I tell it, it's going to sound a bit suggestive and I don't intend it to. There was I, in my Salvation Army uniform and bonnet, out on the street with this young fellow kneeling on the pavement and putting his arm up inside my skirt ... reaching up for the wires, you see ...

Just at that moment there were two women passing on the other side of the road, with their shopping baskets full of groceries. One of the women let out such an 'Oh!', and dropped her basket of groceries ... there were apples and potatoes rolling all down the pavement. 'Good God!' the other woman said. 'Just look at that!' In all the commotion I turned to look at them, and the first woman laughed and said, 'Ho! ho! It's only Thora he's doing it to. So that's all right!'

I've often thought – they can send people into space, land on the moon ... you'd think they could invent something a bit cleverer than having to put a hand up your skirt to fix a mike on, wouldn't you?

Captain Emily Ridley was one of those characters that every actress enjoys playing – because although you laughed at her, you also felt sorry for her. The joke was, although she was a Salvation Army captain she should have been much higher ranking by that stage in her career, and really she was a failure and her superiors were a little embarrassed and ashamed of her, because she was terribly accident-prone. In the story, they decide to put her in charge of her own citadel ... but it's a completely run-down citadel. We found a very shabby, derelict building to film in – there was a little sadness about it, but it had the right atmosphere.

It wouldn't have mattered to her if it had been a hen-house, she was so proud to have been put in charge of her own citadel. Helped by the faithful Alice Meredith, delightfully played by Patsy Rowlands, Emily set about, week after week, to go about doing good, and week after week everything always went wrong, in a funny way of course.

There was one thing about her ... she would talk to the Lord, and ask for help or, if she'd done something wrong, to apologise. So many people wrote to me saying, 'I do that! That's exactly how I talk to the Lord ...' And I do too. I don't mean I talk out loud to the Lord in Sainsbury's so people can hear me, but I do talk to him anywhere I am.

I've always loved the Salvation Army and I'm a great admirer of all the wonderful work they do. Every day, all over the world, thousands of people find themselves in too much trouble to be able to help themselves, and the Lord's own Army is always there to lend a hand.

11

A 'first-class' production

Sometimes you know immediately that a play you're in is going to be a *first-class* production.

I felt really honoured to be asked to be in the Screen Two production of Muriel Spark's *Momento Mori*, because you don't say 'Jack Clayton, the director' you say 'Jack Clayton, the genius' if you've any sense. Mr Clayton treats you as a professional, wouldn't take you on unless you *were* a professional and, I'll tell you something for nothing, even if you weren't when you started, by the time you've worked with him for any length of time – you *are* a professional!

In some ways it was a bit like an old school reunion, all the cast having known each other for so many years. It was a joy even to watch the scenes you weren't in, they were all so good. Michael Hordern – oh, what a great man – Maurice Denham, who I've known for a thousand years, Maggie Smith, Cyril Cusack, Zoë Wanamaker, Stephanie Cole – all marvellous artists – and the wonderful Renee Asherson, who I had last worked with in the days before she married Robert Donat; it was really so nice to be with her again. She's such a dainty little soul. I felt very happy to be playing her maid.

We were filming in an ex-naval hospital that had

been shut down for ages, and it was terribly cold. I was playing the servant, the old family retainer, and I had a long scene in bed in the hospital, with John Wood, playing the Detective, at my bedside. I remember I had a line, 'You knew it was her, didn't you?' It was freezing cold, so I was glad to be in the bed. Jack Clayton was there, wearing the biggest muffler you ever saw in your life round his neck, and as he was standing on the set I said, 'Now how would you like this, Mr de Grundfeld?' and he just looked at me, so I said, 'Well, there are five or six ways I can say this. I can say: "You *knew* it was her ..., didn't you?"

   or: "You knew it was *her* ..., didn't you?"

   or: "*You* knew it was her, didn't you?"

   or: "YOU *KNEW* – IT WAS *HER*! – DIDN'T YOU?"

   or –'

By this time the crew were all laughing, so I said, 'This is a fact – this is a very important line, and there are many, many ways of saying it.'

But it was something even more than all the above that told me I was in a really 'first-class' production ... Stephanie Cole and I were convulsed by this. The toilet was quite a long way away, along a path outside the hospital, towards the end of a block. The first time I wanted to 'go' was during a coffee break – thank heaven – and I said, 'Excuse me getting out of bed, but I'd like to go to the loo.' 'Right!' said someone, who shot off ahead of me. There were some steps down outside, and I saw there was a car there and a chauffeur who opened the door when he saw me, so I said, 'No! I'm not going home. I'm only going to the toilet.' And he said, 'Yes, I know. I'm taking you.'

And, indeed, that is exactly what he was there for –

a chauffeur to drive us to and from the toilet!

I promise you, that has never happened to me in my life, before or since, and you could tell from that alone it really was going to be a *first-class* production.

12

When I grow up ...

I don't think there is a human being who doesn't have childhood ambitions of some sort. From the time we are able to talk we'll say, 'When I grow up I'm going to ...' And we all know people who have worked hard and sacrificed many things to achieve their ambitions.

When I was about six or seven years old I discovered my first ambition – now do pay attention, because this is a three-act play I'm going to tell you about.

Act One: Every Saturday I went to Dugdale's Pork Butchers ... it was a good'un! Lovely smells of roasting pork, meat pies, butter, black puddings – and 'palony'. (Do you remember palony? It was a sort of pork paste filling in a bright red skin like a very thick salami, sold by weight. I haven't seen any for years. In fact I've never seen any in London. I'm not saying there isn't any in London – I don't want dozens of Londoners writing and telling me off, or where I can get it – I'm simply saying *I* haven't seen any.) Now where was I?

Oh, I remember, I was in Dugdale's Pork Butchers. Every Saturday we had what my mother called 'a *bought* lunch'. I know that sounds as though we never bought any other food, but you understand me, don't you? She meant a 'shop' lunch – no cooking at home. My regular order at Dugdale's was: a quarter of boiled ham, a quarter of tongue and two ounces of corned beef.

Act Two: We would eat it with home-made pickled onions and home-made pickled red cabbage and, instead of home-made bread, I would have been to Dora's – the little confectioner two minutes from our house – for six-penny-worth of 'oven-bottom cakes'. For unbelievers, I will explain that an 'oven-bottom cake' was not a cake at all, but rather like a tea-cake, only slightly thicker and larger, and baked in the oven bottom, seven for sixpence. We'd eat them warm, plastered with creamy farm butter bought from the milkman – Ernie Thornton, in case you want to know his name (and not to be confused with Ernie who drove 'the fastest milk-cart in the west' that the wonderful Benny Hill used to sing about).

Act Three: I would go to Newsome's in Euston Road for two chocolate eclairs, two cream horns and two vanilla slices. When the Four Hirds (Dad, Mam, Nev and I) had had a cake each to finish our meal, the two remaining cakes were cut in two and the four pieces would sit there while we thought which half of which cake we would have. What a meal! Menu: Cold cuts (as they say in America) with home-made pickles. Choice of sweets: pastries various. Milk or Tea. It was the same every Saturday, and it was, excuse my plain English, ruddy lovely.

To return to the ambitions, which is what this chapter is supposed to be about, my greatest ambition at that period was ... to make enough money to be able to have as many vanilla slices as I wanted. I love vanilla slices to this day, and I have got enough money to have them as often as I want – so I suppose you could say I have achieved that ambition.

The second was more serious, and came to me when I was about twelve, when we had 'the City of Pompeii' for History one term. I cannot remember ever being so impressed by any period of history. I thought about it for days – weeks – especially the bit about 'And people are still to be seen, covered in ashes and lapilli, sitting eating their meals.' Covered in lava … eating their meals … and dead for years! I nearly drove my brother Nev daft talking about it, asking him questions and badgering him over and over again to explain why the people were sitting eating, and hadn't run away. 'Aw, our kid, do shurrup about bloomin' Pompeii!' he would say, 'It was all so sudden. And they're not still sitting there eating their meals properly now. They're dead. Petrified.' So you can understand, a visit to the city of Pompeii was a 'must' for when I grew up and could see the world.

And yet it was not until 1989 that Scottie and I went to Sorrento, and stayed at the Grand Hotel ExcelsiorVictoria. Scottie had been looking at the diary some time in August and found I had a couple of weeks free the following October. Out came the holiday brochures. 'How about Sorrento? We could stay at the ExcelsiorVictoria – where Jan and I stayed years ago.'

The reason he had stayed there with Jan and without me was because in those days our twelve-year-old daughter was a child film star. (She'll shoot me for saying that, but it's true!) She was in *Helen of Troy* and was filming in Rome for about three months, and of

course her father was with her – not in the film, I mean
– as chaperone, companion and general looker-after.
They suddenly found they had a week or so free, so
they decided to spend it in Sorrento, and booked into
the Grand Hotel ExcelsiorVictoria (what a mouthful
this hotel name is becoming!).

'Of course, it will have altered a lot. But it's a five-
star hotel and sounds all right. What do you think?' I
was stitching a button on his blazer. 'I think – yes,
let's,' I said, as I snipped the cotton after the comple-
tion of the button sewing (with shank, kindly note). I
was also thinking that Sorrento is very near Pompeii –
my childhood ambition was at long last about to be
fulfilled. So to Sorrento we went.

As we arrived in our room at the hotel I asked
Scottie if he thought it had changed much since his last
visit. 'Well, I can't remember every detail after forty
odd years,' Scottie said, 'But ... ' at that moment he was
interrupted by a waiter gliding into our room with a
bottle of very cold champagne and two glasses, who
silently opened the bottle, poured out the icy golden
liquid and handed us a frosted glass each, and glided
out. 'No, it hasn't altered up to now!' said Scottie, as
we raised our glasses and wished each other a happy
holiday.

Anyway, here I was at last – nearly eighty years old,
excited as a child about getting my first glimpse of
Pompeii, that long-imagined place – and just a walk
away from our hotel.

Oh dear. Everyone, just everyone, advised me
against visiting Pompeii, because of my arthritis. The
ground is very uneven, and there's a hill to be
climbed to get to the entrance. I was determined to go

anyway, until I thought of Scottie, who would have to assist me every minute. He said it would be no trouble, but was still afraid it would be too much for me. So, I thought, 'Go on, Thor. Get back in your cheese. I'll keep my own picture of what it all looks like. Sorry Pompeii!'

I'll just write Pompeii on my very small list of things I've always wanted – and never got – and never will.

And why should I? I've had everything that matters – the love of a wonderful husband and family and the love of my friend upstairs, the good Lord. I don't even care about my old wish list any longer, but here it is in its entirety:

1. Eat as many vanilla slices as I want
2. Visit Pompeii
3. Live in a cottage with a thatched roof and inglenook fireplace
4. Play Mrs Pankhurst
5. Own a mink coat and hat

1. Well – of course – I can afford to eat all the vanilla slices I want now, and I still love 'em … but not being seven or eight years old any longer, I never want more than one.
2. Pompeii. It would have to be from a helicopter for me to see it now … but I have such a wonderful picture of it in my imagination, I think it might spoil it to see the real thing.
3. I realise a thatched roof is imposs. Dangerous and madly expensive to insure, but I have now got a lovely eighteenth-century cottage with a big stone fireplace,

big enough to display my collection of copper and brass. And in these days of central heating – who could want for more?

4. I'm too old to play Mrs Pankhurst now. And with all the wonderful parts Alan Bennett has written for me over the past twenty years – why do anything less?

5. Mink coat and hat – got 'em! Can't wear 'em (in case somebody chucks an egg at me).

13

'Bluddy Love'

This chapter is all about love – we'll only come to the 'bluddy' bit at the end. Every mother, grandmother, auntie, sister knows that there are so many sorts of love. It's worth your sitting down with a cup of coffee after your lunch and having a think, 'Just a minute ... I'll have a count ... how many sorts of love are there?'

I mean, the love you have for your mother is different from the love you have for your father. The love you have for your brother is different from for your sister or best friends.

I've always thought – and you may agree with this or not, and if you don't agree, it gives you a chance to turn to your friend and say, 'Do you see what she says? That's not right ...' But I think that fathers are inclined to lean to the daughter in the family, and the mother, I am sure, leans to the boy.

I can remember this very vividly. We were an extremely happy household – and you must be fed up of hearing me say that – but my brother Neville was a year and nine months older than I was, and my mother adored him. Bit of a strong word, but my mother loved my brother very much. She loved me too, but I said to her one day, 'You love our Neville more than you love me, don't you?' She looked at me, did my mother, with the actress's face, and she said, 'God forgive you for saying that!' It was as though I'd accused her of murder or something. And she said – I always remember the word she used, because when I was young and I got hold of a new word I didn't understand, the moment I understood it (or thought I understood it) I would use it a lot. She said, 'I don't love Neville one *iota* more than I love you.'

I was using 'iota' in the wrong place for about a month after that, because I liked it. 'She did not leave an iota of food,' and my mother would say, 'Oh no, no, Thora, that's not right!' I remember the word 'adamant'. When I heard the word adamant I thought, 'Oh, that's nice ... No, I'm *adamant*.' Adamant. Iota. There are some lovely words in the language, you know.

But I digress. Love is the word we're talking about. My mother said to me, 'Don't you ever say that again, Thora. I love you both equally.' And of course she did. But I think there is a thing – is 'genetically' the right word? I mean, my father, if I was out a bit late – of course it's so old-fashioned if one talks about it now, 'obedience', but if my parents said to me, 'Right, be in for ten o'clock' I had no reason to think 'Well, five past will do. Six past will do'; I was in for ten o'clock. You were in those days. But I know that if ever I *was* a minute or two late, my mother would be saying 'She's late ...' but my father would say, 'We-ell – she could have been ...' and always make an excuse for me. And my mother, if my brother was ever late, would say, 'Well, Jimmy, he's a lot of friends. They'll be talking politics round the lamp.' That was the lamp in our street. I tell you, this country was run from 'round the

66

lamp' opposite our house. It was an alternative government.

You feel another kind of love for your friends and neighbours. There's even a love you have for an animal, a pet dog or cat. Children love their dolls and soft toys. Then there's the difference between loving somebody, and being 'in love'. There's the times you think you are 'in love', but you're not, like, as in my case, with some of the boys you meet before you get married. Then when you do get married, that's a different love altogether.

When you are a woman and you have your baby, well, that is a love you can't describe. Mother love is a love on its own. I remember when they said to me – 'Here's your baby,' and all in a second thinking a thousand things that every mother thinks, 'Oh, she's mine! Oh, isn't she wonderful?'

I would like to say that I am one of the best mothers in the world. I would *like* to say it, when, forgive me, really I am a bluddy nuisance! This is the truth. There is my daughter, Jan, a grown-up married woman with two children of her own, and they're grown-ups now too. She's a very capable, very loving woman, and I know when I'm ill there's no one I'd rather have around than Jan. But if she's on her own in the house, I'll ring her up about three times that night and I'll make an excuse, although I know she knows perfectly well that I'm really thinking, 'Are you all right?' Of course she's all right! She's much more capable of looking after herself than I am. I'll say to her later, when I see her, 'You must excuse me if I'm a nuisance, but you know it's because I love you.' And she'll give me a lovely look and say, 'I know it's because you love me!' And she laughs.

Sometimes when you love someone, it's hard to say it. Lancashire is a county full of very loving and lovable people. I say that because I know Lancashire and Lancashire people probably better than I know anyone else. And so often they'll say something that sounds *so unkind* – but which is sincerely meant for loving kindness. Here are just two short examples I can think of, just to give you a little laugh before you close the book and go to sleep.

One was when I was in a bad car accident in about 1957, and more or less went through the windscreen. I was in hospital, with my face about a foot wide – blue, yellow, pink – and my mouth was standing up like a figure one, so you might know I really didn't look too pretty! A lady came in, with her niece, who was going into the next bed to have her appendix out. I don't think the girl was nervous, only her auntie kept saying 'There's nothing to worry about, Nellie! Don't be worried.' Well, the girl *wasn't* worried, but after about fifteen times of hearing this, she began to look very worried. Auntie was fussing around and she put five brown fruit bags on the locker between my bed and the girl's and said, 'Now, Nellie, you won't be able to eat these until tomorrow. They'll not let you eat any of these tonight.' Then the nurse came along and said, 'I'm afraid I'll have to ask you to go now, as we've to serve the teas, and it isn't really visiting day.'

(And that's another thing – pardon me just coming off the story for a minute – there used to be 'Visiting Hours: 2 – 3, Wednesday and Saturday'. Nowadays you can visit someone in hospital every day at nine in the morning if you want, and stay all day. Whether that's better or worse, I don't know.)

Anyhow, Auntie started to put on her left glove, getting ready to go. I say this because I want you to visualise this woman with her glove, pulling the fingers on, and as she did so she looked round and noticed me in the next bed. As I say, I was not a pretty sight, and she said, 'Is it ... Thora?' I gave her a sort of nod, and she said, 'Hough! Dear me! What a sight! What a sample!' Then she leaned over me, still pulling her glove on, and the entire ward must have heard her as she whispered very loudly, right in my ear 'What a good job you were never good-looking before!'

Now that sounds cruel, I know, but it isn't. She was meaning to be very kind. And if you work it out – it *was* a good job I wasn't good-looking before!

The other little example I'll tell you about was when I was in Morecambe to play at the theatre in Bank Holiday week. It really was, as we say up there, 'raining stair rods'. I was staying with some friends who had a very nice flat looking out onto the promenade, and on this particular morning I was looking out and there was not a soul to be seen. Just an empty prom, empty beach and driving rain.

Then into view comes a fellow in one of those grey macintoshes that you could roll up and put in an envelope. They were very popular when they first came out. He's got new white plimsolls on – you could tell they were bought for his holiday. An open-necked cricket shirt. And a cap. About two yards behind him trails a little child – I would say two or three years old – in a little red mac and sou'wester. He's got his beach bucket in his hand, and a tin- or iron-ended spade, not a wooden spade, which he's trailing along the ground. The window I was watching them from was open at the top, and I could hear this child's spade scraping along. The man was walking in front, head down, funeral pace, and he suddenly turned round and looked at this kid, trailing along in the pouring rain, and he was fed up, and he said, 'Eeeeee! Come on, bluddy love!'

I thought to myself – the affection in that – 'Come on, bluddy love!' I could just imagine the young mother sitting in the holiday lodgings, with a paperback novel, and the child going mad since breakfast 'Are we going on the sands? Are we going to the sea?' And she must have said, 'Oh, Edwin – take him and let him have a walk along!'

So you see, that's Lancashire folk for you – 'Come on, bluddy love!'

14

Twice nightly

For many years on a summer Sunday evening you had to make up your mind: 'Now shall I watch Thora on the BBC? Or Sir Harry on ITV?' We both had audiences of six or seven or more million viewers – so that wasn't bad going for the 'God slot', was it? Fourteen million or more people between us, watching religious programming.

Harry Secombe and I had first met years ago, even long before we worked together at the London Palladium in 1966 when Harry was presenting a show called *London Laughs*. I had to turn down a part in a West End play to be in it – and thank goodness I did – thirty-two weeks, twice nightly and three shows on a Saturday ... wonderful! At that time I was in a television comedy series with Freddie Frinton, *Meet the Wife*, so Freddie and I acted out an episode from the show on stage.

The second act opened with a big cockney scene. Harry and I rode on stage dressed as a Pearly King and Queen in a lovely little cart, pulled along by a very lovable little donkey who was brought to the side of the stage just a few minutes before he was needed. Of course we all had tit-bits for him before he went on stage. It never went to his head. He was the dearest little thing and – please note, *James Tarbuck!* – I can't remember the donkey *ever* misbehaving on stage! In fact, my greatest wish from then on was to be able to ride in a donkey cart – in real life, not on stage – a wish that was to be granted nearly thirty years later – but that's another story.

Well, years rolled by, and soon after I started presenting *Praise Be!* Harry began presenting *Highway*. So now we were both doing religious programmes, with interviews and hymns, and I'm told that any time they had to stop the filming on *Highway* for a few moments (as you often have to do if an aeroplane goes overhead, drowning out the sound) Harry would unfailingly look up and say, 'There goes Thora Hird in her spy-helicopter again!'

But it was always a friendly rivalry, and eventually the *Highway* team asked me if I would come on Sir Harry's programme, during a time when *Praise Be!* wasn't on the air. I very happily joined him on the sands at Grange, across the bay from Morecambe, where I read 'Footprints' – a beautiful piece about how God carries you through the hardest parts of your life.

It was a beautiful day, and I read it to the best of my ability, and when it got to lunchtime Harry had to be driven off to the airport while I stayed for lunch with the director. As Harry was leaving – I can see him now, hanging out of the window at the back – he shouted out, 'Here! Thora! Don't forget to ask me to be on *Praise Be-e-e!*' And from the busy pavement outside the restaurant I shouted back, 'No! I will! I will! I promise you, Harry, I will!'

And indeed I did. The trouble was, *Highway* was

always on the air during the six weeks in the summer when *Praise Be!* was on. The strange thing was, Liz Barr, who I work with as often as I can when I'm doing my religious programmes and books, was then with the BBC producing *Praise Be!*, and her husband Andrew Barr was with ITV, producing *Highway*. So there was a man and wife, sitting round their kitchen table in their cottage of an evening, working on their scripts, his for Harry and hers for me. Unfortunately even they couldn't get the two companies to agree to let Harry come on my show, because it would have meant that if the audience were watching Harry on *Praise Be!*, they wouldn't be watching him on *Highway*, you see. So that was the reason he never came on. It was a shame, because I would have loved to have had him on my show. He's a very funny, lovable man, with great faith.

So it all goes to show, as someone once wrote in my autograph book when I was a little girl – it was purple kid leather with 'Autographs' in gilt on the front cover – 'The scene is set, the lights are on, the stage is all aglow, but what may happen behind the scenes – only the artists know!'

15

Cream Crackers

In 1987 the BBC presented a series of Alan Bennett's plays under the title *Talking Heads*. Now I've always enjoyed saying Alan's words, but I can remember this time, when I first read *Cream Cracker Under the Settee*, thinking, 'This one is going to be difficult to play without crying.' Among the many things that my father taught me about the business – and, Heaven knows, he taught me all the important things – one was: if you show too much emotion, you won't glean a lot. And it's true is that. Show too many tears and you don't get the people watching you as moved as you will if you fight it a little.

On the first day of rehearsals I got to about page eleven and I could hardly speak it, I was so upset. I apologised through my tears to the director, Stuart Burge. I said, 'I'm awfully sorry. I won't be like this by Friday.' He was blowing his nose, and he said, 'Won't you? I still will!'

It was a forty-four-minute play, or monologue, and Scottie, who was always at the back of me about everything – and I so often wonder what I would have done without him ... well, I know what I would have done without him, probably – nothing ... Anyhow, as it was my habit to get up first in the morning and go straight in the bathroom and turn the taps on, Scottie said to me, 'When you get up in the morning, don't turn your bathwater on. Let's get on the book.' (Meaning – study the words.) Which is what we did.

I said to Scottie on the second morning, 'Would you like a bit of a bet, for fun?' And he said, 'A bet? What about?' And I said, 'That I'll know it in six mornings.' To which that lovely face looked at me and he said, 'Well, of course you'll know it! That's what they're paying you for, to know it!'

Anyhow, little did I think it was going to do all for me that it did. It's a wonderful play to do, a wonderful part for any actress.

But here is an interesting thing: *Cream Cracker* was a play – it was *a play* – about an elderly citizen who doesn't want to be made to go into a home for old people. But it must have seemed very real to a lot of people – I had hundreds of letters afterwards, and amongst them there were at least three I will never forget. One of them, I can see the paper now – avocado, deckle-edged, expensive, *beautiful* notepaper – it said, 'Dear Thora Hird, It is three o'clock in the morning and I haven't been to sleep yet. I saw you last night in *Cream Cracker Under the Settee*, and I *beseech* you, now that our children are all married and gone away, *please* come and live with us! We have a large house in the country. We live very nicely. You are so welcome!'

And I thought, 'A woman like this must *know* – it is a play.' Anyhow, I got through about another fifty letters, and I opened one, and this was on lined pad paper. It said, 'Dear Thora Hird, We only have a little house, but we have a spare bedroom. Don't you go

into that Stafford House.' And there was another very
nice one and it said, 'I couldn't go to sleep and my
husband said, "Are you still awake? What's the
matter?" and I said, "Oh, I do hope in the morning
they notice she hasn't taken the milk in!"' I'm not
making fun – it's a compliment really, that they think
you're so good you must be for real. Or, at any rate,
they think you are for real, whether they think you're
good or not.

The play opens with my character, Doris, getting up
off the floor to sit in a chair because she has fallen off
the buffet she had climbed on to get down a wedding
picture of herself and her husband Wilfred, to dust it,
because she has a council cleaning lady, Zulema, who
she doesn't think dusts properly. She says: 'Zulema
doesn't dust. She half-dusts. I know when a place isn't
clean.' Later, when she's down on the floor again, she
sees a cream cracker under the settee, where Zulema
has also failed to clean properly. And by the end of the
evening, she dies.

Mr Bennett knows how to write that sort of thing.
You saw the shadow of a policeman through the glass
on the front door, and he calls out:

'Hello. Hello. Are you all right?' And she says, 'No. I'm
    all right.'
'Are you sure?'
'Yes.'
'Your light was off.'
'I was having a nap.'
'Sorry. Take care.'
'Thank you.' She calls again. 'Thank you.' Long pause.
'You've done it now, Doris. Done it now, Wilfred.'

76

I couldn't get into a taxi-cab, I couldn't anything without somebody mentioning *Cream Cracker*. People stopped me in the street and said, 'Why didn't you call back to him? Why didn't you tell him you were on the floor?' And it was no good my saying to people, 'I didn't say it like that because it wasn't in the play.'

But it did so much for me, that play. However old I was, however long I'd been in the business, it did me so much good and, of course, it got me a BAFTA.

The BAFTA ceremony is like all those things you see on television, where they read out three or four names in each of the different categories: 'And they are: Dee, dee, dee and dee ... and the winner is: ...'

I was invited to the dinner, but I'd been invited many times before and never won anything. On this occasion I was a long way from the stage at Grosvenor House, at a table with Jan and Scottie. Young David Dimbleby made a speech, requesting that when they received their award people shouldn't make a speech thanking their uncles and their cousins and everybody for helping them to act.

So there we are, having our dinner, and it comes to the Drama award and, after they'd shown little bits of the various *Talking Heads* plays, I sat there, being quite used to other years never getting any BAFTA award, and then Peter Davidson from *All Creatures Great and Small* said, 'And the winner is ... Thora Hird in *Cream Cracker Under the Settee*.'

Well! I'll never forget that moment – they gave me a standing ovation. It was probably because I was a lot older than the other actresses, but everyone stood up and cheered and whistled, and it made me feel marvellous.

Getting to that platform to receive it, however, is even more difficult than winning the BAFTA in the first place. The chairs are so close together round the tables, and you're going 'Excuse me', 'Do you mind?', 'Could I get through?' And it seemed to take me a year to get there. However, eventually I got to the stage and remembered what Mr Dimbleby had said, so when young Davidson handed me the BAFTA – they're very heavy, by the way – I was going to leg it, but he sort of kissed me, near me ear. Well, that's what I thought, anyway, that he was kissing me near my ear. Really, he was whispering 'They would like you to say a few words.' So I handed him the BAFTA back, because it was really too heavy for me to hold, and I said a few words, covering a lot of track with it. I told them about my very first stage appearance, when I was eight weeks old, being carried on by my mother. And I could truthfully say that that was the only part I ever got due to influence! I thanked Stuart Burge, and Alan Bennett, of course, who got a big cheer and a round of applause. And I staggered back to my seat with my first BAFTA, a very proud and happy woman.

When I was very young in the business, as long as people were saying, 'Thank you very much' and 'That was very good' I felt that was reward enough, and I certainly never thought I would come to this time of my life and start receiving awards like the BAFTA for drama, the Pye award for Comedy, the Royal Variety Club award for my contribution to the world of entertainment, another special silver BAFTA – just for being Thora Hird I think that was – and become the first woman member of the Royal Television Society's Hall of Fame – elected on 15 May, 1993 ... and several other things, like the Help the Aged and Tunstall Golden Award, and a Woman of the Year award – but they're not really for acting. Of course I'm proud of them. I'm not one of those actors who uses them for a door stop or hides them away in a cupboard and pretends they mean nothing – I polish them lovingly and keep them on the sideboard.

That reminds me, I have an old pot hot-water bottle from when I was a child, and an old flat iron, and I noticed the other night that Jan has put a pot hot-water bottle as one door stop, and a flat iron as another, so those are two ideas I'm going to pinch. But I can assure you that no BAFTA of mine is going to end up a door stop!

16

Alan Bennett

So many people ask me, 'What's Alan Bennett like?'
It's very difficult, really, to describe Alan. He talks to
me as though I was his grandmother, but I wouldn't
say I knew him very well personally, only through
acting what he writes. Even then you don't always
know whether he loves or hates the character he's
written for you to play.

Of course, he is a very funny man. He sent me a
postcard one day, from Yorkshire, where he lives
when he's not in London. It said, 'Just come back for
the day to put a new lavatory seat on. Love, Alan.'
That's Alan, you see. I had another postcard, also from
Yorkshire, and it was just like a postcard you'd get
from anyone, and I read it and thought, 'There's nothing funny on this postcard. It's not like Alan, this.'
And then I turned the postcard over, and it was a
beautiful picture of the Yorkshire moors, and in the
corner it said, 'Soldier's Bottom'. So then I knew why
he'd sent it.

There was one morning at rehearsal. He arrived.
His clothes are very good but I can't say he's the
smartest man I've ever seen in my life. He nearly
always wears a good suit – but often with a pair of
shabby grey cricket boots. He says, 'Well, they're

comfortable.' This day he had on a rather beautiful overcoat – a very good coat, although I did notice the sleeves went down to his fingertips. When we were going home he was putting it on and I said to him, 'That's a nice coat, Alan. Is it new?' He said proudly, 'I've just bought it. Do you like it?' I said, 'Well, I do ... I'd like it even better on somebody a bit bigger than you.' He said, 'It was in a sale.' He was so proud of it because he'd bought it in a sale, and he thought that that excused everything, whether it fitted him or not. And I thought, 'Aren't you lovely! You can afford fifty overcoats like that, to fit you. But because this was in a sale ...' I'm a bit like this myself. Of course, he's a northerner too, and we're all a bit careful.

He really makes me laugh, especially when he's telling stories about when he was a little boy, with his mother and father and aunties. He told me a story about being on top of a bus with his auntie and, as they passed the gasworks in Leeds, she said to him, 'Alan – that is the biggest gasworks in England.' And he said to me, 'Well, you know, Thora, when you're about ten you're not that interested in the gasworks, whether it is the biggest one or not,' so he just glanced at it but didn't say anything, and after about another minute or two his auntie sort of straightened herself up and said, 'And *I* – know – the manager!'

In one of the plays I did for him I had one of the funniest lines – as far as I am concerned – that I have ever had to say. It was a play called *Me, I'm Afraid of Virginia Woolf*. In it I have a son, Trevor, at the Polytechnic. We're in the cafeteria at the Poly, having a cup of tea, and I'm beseeching him to say that he is at 'College'. You know the sort of woman.

'Well, you could *say* you were at College.'

'I can't, Mother. I'm at the Polytechnic.'

'Well, it's the same thing.'

'No it isn't.'

In the conversation, in the play, he happens to mention the word 'lesbian' and you know by my face that my character does not know what a lesbian is. And she keeps asking him, 'But what is a lesbian?' and he doesn't answer, but eventually he gets so fed up he says to her, 'Oh, mother! They are women who sleep together.' She looks him straight in the face, and says

'Well, that's nothing! I slept with your Auntie Phyllis all during the air-raids!'

That's the line. I really do think it's funny. Alan can write four words and link them together and they can be funny, or they can be very sad. I remember a speech I had to make about losing a baby in *Cream Cracker Under the Settee*:

'I wanted to call it John. But the nurse said it wasn't worth calling anything, and had we any newspaper.'

The sadness in that. Telling you what happened in so few words, without ever mentioning the word 'miscarriage'. And later in the same speech she says, 'And Wilfred said, "Oh yes, she saves newspapers. She saves shoe boxes as well."' (He means for a coffin, you see. You know at once.) She goes on, 'I don't think Wilfred cared very much about losing the baby, because it was then he talked about us getting a dog ...'

You can see the fellow, can't you? It was at that point, at rehearsals, that I said to Stuart Burge, 'I hate bloody Wilfred! I don't know what I married him for!'

I think perhaps the reason I've enjoyed working

with Alan so much is because, in my own small way, I do the same as him. Behind his work are all the characters he's been listening to and conversations he's overheard, and behind my acting are the people I grew up with, who came round to our house and who came in the shop when I was working in the Co-op. That was when I saw and overheard so many funny things that people did, and where I learned many little 'bits of business', little things you can do that say almost more than a page of words about what the character is like.

Alan has a brilliant ear for how people say things, especially north country people. Now, we're all guilty sometimes of not sticking exactly to a script, especially when it comes to little words like the conjunctions. Every actor and actress has at some time altered the words a tiny bit to make them easier to say. But if Alan has put 'but' you say 'but', you don't say 'and' or 'if'. He'll say immediately 'That's a "but".' He's never unpleasant about it. He'll just be walking about with his hands in his pockets at the far end of the studio, and he'll say quietly, 'that's a "but".' He knows what he's written, what he wants you to say, and it's so good you want to say it right.

If anybody thinks I've said all this because I'm hoping that he'll ask me to work with him again ... they'd be quite right.

17

Russell Harty

Television critics were never fair to him. They could never understand his popularity, but as far as the public were concerned he was one of the most entertaining chat-show hosts in the business, mainly because he had the cheek of the devil and didn't mind asking anybody anything. I went on his show three or four times and he always used to say, 'I'm going to ask you about that time when you were in hospital after the car accident,' and I always said, 'Oh no, I told that last time I was on, Russell!' And he always said, 'Never mind, it's worth telling again!' So I did! And now I've told you about it again in this book, haven't I?

Things never went quite right when Russell was around. I don't mean he was accident-prone, or anything, but things always seemed to go a bit askew. He was a very good friend of Alan Bennett's – they had met at university, I believe, and stayed friends ever since. While we were doing Alan's play *Me, I'm Afraid of Virginia Woolf* in Yorkshire, Russell was there watching – and when we were doing the scene I've told you about, in the Polytechnic cafeteria, Russell was sitting at the far end, and when I said my line 'That's nothing ... I slept with your Auntie Phyllis all during the air-raids,' he laughed so much the director had to ask him to leave.

Russell was driving back to London the next day by car, and Alan said to me, 'Why don't you go back with Russell? You'll be company for each other ...' So I gave my train ticket to the stage manager (she said she would find somebody who would use it) and I set off with Russell in the car.

We were going along and he said to me, 'We'll stop at –' do you know, I just can't think of the place where it was – 'because, there is a very good restaurant called The Vineyard.' I said, 'Oh, great.' And we arrived at – you see, I'm no good with maps and so on, so I still don't know where it was – but we arrived in the high street of the town where this restaurant was, and there was a man coming along with a dog and Russell said, 'Ask this fellow if he knows where it is.' So I put the window down and said, 'Excuse me, sir, could you direct us to a restaurant called The Vineyard?' and I notice out of the corner of my eye while I'm saying this that Russell is rooting around for something on the floor of the car, his side, so his face isn't showing. I thought, 'Oh yes? *Oh* yes!' So I said to the gentleman with the dog, 'Only Mr – *Russell Harty* – and I are going there for lunch.' And the man said, 'Well, no, I don't know where it is' and went on. Then I saw a girl coming towards us with a perambulator – Russell is still craning his head round so no one will recognise him. I put down the window again and asked her if she knew where it was. 'Oh, is that Russell Harty?' she said immediately. She didn't know where the restaurant was either, but there was another lady coming along, extremely well dressed, and I leant out and said, 'Excuse me, madam, could you direct me to a restaurant called The Vineyard!' and she said, 'Oh! Thora Hird! Oh what a pleasure to meet you!' and I said, 'Thank you ... and could you tell us ...?' and she said, 'And is that Mr Harty? Oh, fancy meeting two of you at the same time ... Oh, this is such a surprise. Are you visiting the town for long? Are you making a programme here?'

'No. Yes. Thank you. We're just passing through. But have you any idea where the restaurant is?'

'Yes' she said, 'You're right outside it!' And we were! We had been parked right outside this bloomin' restaurant the whole time. Somehow that was typical of how things happened when you were with Russell.

God rest him, he was a good friend and a very lovable man.

18

The Queen and I

On 29 November, 1990, I took a lot of care getting ready. I wasn't really nervous – anxious, yes – excited? Yes. I hired a dignified car and chauffeur in matching grey (well, the car was, and his uniform was). I arrived at her house exactly on time – to the minute. There were only eight of us for lunch, six guests, our hostess and her sister:

Her Majesty the Queen, and Her Royal Highness Princess Margaret.

A lot of funny things happen to me, I'm very happy to say, and I know a lot of funny people. And like everybody else that's human, I'm wrong as often as I'm right. But this is an occasion when I was wrong ... or right ... but read on and take your choice!

I had come home one afternoon in October. Scottie was just about to lay the telephone on its cradle and he said, 'Oh, just a minute, she's here,' and held the telephone up again. As I went over to him I mouthed, 'Who is it?' and he shook his head to say that he didn't know.

Now at this point I need to interject something. You all know Michael Jayston, the very clever actor? Some years previously we had both been together on location filming for a BBC drama series, *Flesh and Blood*, in which he played one of my grandsons and I was the eighty-year-old matriarch of a cement family. I came down to the hotel dining room one morning and there was a letter for me from some retired Major or Colonel, asking me to come out with him for a drink. He'd fallen on hard times since leaving the army, otherwise he'd have asked me out to dinner. I thought, 'What a shame!' I wasn't going to go or anything, but I thought, 'How sad.' So I was telling Michael about this letter, over breakfast, and I was saying 'Isn't it sad? When they've done so much for their country, you know ...' And I saw his face twitch, just the slightest in the world. I said, 'It's a proper letter, isn't it?' He said, 'Oh, it's sure to be! You will go, won't you?' So then I knew ... he'd written it. Because Michael is a great man for playing practical jokes on people, but they never hurt anybody.

So back to the morning of the telephone call. When this modulated voice said, 'Miss Hird? This is the Controller of the Queen's Household' I thought, 'Oh yes, I bet it is! Michael Jayston! Ha-ha!' But instead of saying, 'Come off it, Michael' I thought, 'I'll enjoy this performance for a bit,' and then this *beautifully* modulated voice, far too good to be anyone's but an actor's, told me that Her Majesty was desirous of me going to have lunch with her ... I thought, 'Come off it' – I'm sure you'd have thought the same. Then when he said, 'And we realise what a busy lady you are, so there are three possible dates ...' Well, I could just hear the Queen saying, 'Tell Thora, I'm ironing on Tuesday, and I've a bit of baking to do on Wednesday, but any Thursday ...' And I thought, 'All right,

Michael. But go on ...' So I kept up with it and I said, 'Well it's only Thursday, really, that I'm free.' To which the gentleman thanked me very much and said that I would be further advised later on. So as I hung the telephone up Scottie said, 'Who was it?' and I said, 'It was Michael bloomin' Jayston ... The Queen wants me to have lunch with her ... I don't think!' I added, 'He is a scream, isn't he?'

In the middle of the following week a very large gilt-edged invitation card arrived which informed me that Her Majesty the Queen was desirous of me having lunch with her on Thursday, two weeks ahead of when the card arrived. Well I really was, I think the expression at the moment is 'gob-smacked.' I wrote back immediately.

At the big gates of Buckingham Palace, as you are all aware, there is often a uniformed policeman at each side. I'd heard on the early morning news that the Ambassador of Turkey was to be received by the Queen – that day. When I'd heard it I'd thought, 'Hold on! Jayston hasn't gone to the expense of having a *card* printed as well, has he? Because if she's receiving the Ambassador of Turkey ...' As we got near, we saw the procession leaving the palace – we'd already been in a back street, killing seven minutes because we were early – and as we arrived at the gates one of the policemen put his hand on top of the car, looked in and said,

'Oh! Hallo, Thora. Go right in.'

This is the truth! I couldn't believe it! At Buckingham Palace ... 'Hallo, Thora ... Go right in ...' The chauffeur said to him, 'How about the parking?' And he said, 'It's all right. There's only six people today.' And all the time I'm saying to myself, 'Hallo, Thora ... Go right in ...'

Anyway, the gentleman with the beautifully modulated voice who I had spoken to on the telephone, who was *not* Michael Jayston, of course, was about four steps down on a side entrance, and in I went. There were two people already there. One was professor Sir Magdi Yacoub, the great man who does the heart transplants, and the other was the man who was for so many years the voice of tennis, Dan Maskell. I was taken over to Dan Maskell, who I already knew, but I hadn't before met the Doctor, so I was very pleased and proud to meet him. The next person to arrive was a Dame, not of the theatre, of industry, and still to arrive was a Romanian author (who *nobody* knew, so we all made a bit of a fuss of him), and the head of the Baltic Exchange.

So it was all very pleasant, the footmen wandering about offering everybody cigarettes, which nobody took. We had a nice sherry, and all had little bits of chat with one another. And suddenly the Master of Ceremonies announced that he did wish to apologise for Her Majesty being a moment or two late, but she had been receiving the Turkish Ambassador. At that point four little corgis ran in, and I thought, 'She'll be here in a minute.' And she was.

She was very kind to us all. We'd formed a row, without being told, out of respect, because we felt that was what we ought to do. She asked me what I was doing at the moment, and I said, 'Well, Your Majesty, we've finished another batch of *Last of the Summer Wine* last night, and put the Christmas one "in the can".' And she smiled and said, 'Oh, when does it come out? My mother never misses one.' So that was nice, wasn't it?

Princess Margaret joined us for lunch. It was all very beautiful – a wonderful experience. The Baltic Exchange asked me how my beautiful daughter was, and said, 'I was so in love with her when I was fifteen!' You like to hear these things, you know, when you're a mother. The whole thing was like going to have lunch with a relative you were very fond of. And of course – the grub was good.

When you hear me say so often how proud I am of being a Lancastrian, you've to excuse me, because I am, and of course the Queen herself is Duke of Lancaster. That sounds wrong, but it's right.

We were in America some years ago, Scottie and I, and Jan was giving a formal dinner party in a restaurant. There were nine tables of people, including quite a few English friends who were staying, and the British Ambassador, who Jan knew very well, a charming man; his wife was a Lancastrian so Jan put me at one table, the Ambassador's wife at another, herself at another, and so on, so that there was at least one Lancastrian at each table. When it was time for the Loyal Toast, the British Ambassador stood up and said, 'I would ask you to be upstanding to drink the health of Her Majesty, Queen Elizabeth the Second ...' and as we all pushed back our chairs and stood up, he went on 'Duke of Lancaster'. So we all drank the toast and then sat down. Opposite me was sitting the lady who owned the Beverly Hills Hotel, and she said, 'Thora, who is the Dook of Lancaster?' On my left was Elm Williams, head of Twentieth-Century Fox at that time, and he said, 'Who's the Dook of Lancaster, Thora?' I wasn't going to say, straight off, because I thought it would be more fun to keep them guessing. And all round the room you could hear this buzz going round all the tables – 'Who's the Dook of Lancaster?' Some clever dick at another table said, 'It's Philip.' So I said, 'Oh no it isn't.' But I still wouldn't say, and Group Captain Leonard Cheshire, who founded the Cheshire Homes, was on my right, falling about as everyone was arguing about 'Who's the Dook of Lancaster?' Eventually we told them that the Queen herself is the Duke of Lancaster, because whoever is on the throne of England, whoever they are, even if they are a dog or a cat, they are also the Duke of Lancaster. I'll never forget that night – the wonder and laughter about this Duke of Lancaster – I think it made them think that the British are completely mad.

The day after we got back to London, shortly after that night, was the day that Prince Charles and Diana announced their engagement. There was a Lancastrian occasion in one of the City Halls, and the Queen came and we gave her the usual big sheaf of red roses, the red rose of Lancashire. As she stopped to speak to me along the line, I said I had just returned from America and that we had offered the Loyal Toast while we were there, and she looked at me so nicely and said, 'I should think they find that rather peculiar, don't they?' And I said, 'Not half so peculiar as you being the Dook of Lancaster!' and she nearly dropped her sheaf of roses she laughed so much!

19

D. Litt.

I couldn't get the velvet cap on right – none of us could ... Oh well. I was a bit disappointed that I hadn't had a little more time to fiddle with it, but we were all being bustled along at such a rate into the procession. Mind you, the Chancellor had got her velvet cap on beautifully – but then, she also had a beautiful face to go under the beautifully put-on cap. I said to her later, at the lunch, 'Look how your cap looks! How beautiful! I hadn't time to put mine on properly. But you would know exactly how to put yours on – this was the wonderful thing about your mother, she was everybody's idea of a princess and she always wore her hats so beautifully!'

Yes! I was talking to our lovely Princess Alexandra. Do you remember her mother, the Duchess of Kent, and how beautifully she wore those brimmed hats? Oh, I do.

Never mind the cap ... off we go. There must have been more than a thousand students seated in the hall as we proceeded to the platform.

We hadn't been settled for very long before a very brilliant gentleman stood up and read pages and pages – all about me! I didn't realise there was so much of interest to tell about me. Then I was called to approach Princess Alexandra and (I was going to say 'before you could say Jack Robinson' but it was rather longer than that) ... anyway, by the time I sat down again I was a D. Litt. or, to put it in full, a Doctor of Letters of the University of Lancaster. Never mind my velvet cap being askew – no woman who had left school at fourteen without an any-level to her name could have been prouder.

Earlier that morning, when I was being driven to the Graduation Hall in Lancaster to receive my honorary degree accompanied by Scottie and Jan, we passed a building that made me go 'Heee-aaah!' (If you want to make that noise – just take a long intake of breath expressing surprise, shock, delight and a flood of memories!). We had just passed the Ashton Hall, Lancaster ... where the Lancaster District Co-op, where I worked as a cashier for ten years, held their annual Dinner and Dance ... tickets half a crown.

I had gone one year with my best friend Peggy wearing a new ball gown (made for me by Doris Brown from further down our street) in eau-de-nil satin, low-waisted, a skirt with four handkerchief points and about a ten-inch deep piece of georgette round the bottom. I can see it now. I do hope you can visualise it. Sounds 'orrible, doesn't it? Really it was quite pretty, and it was my first proper ball gown and I thought it was beautiful. I wore real silk stockings and brocade evening shoes in pale pink and green ... *eau-de-nil*, white gloves, and a little evening bag with a lace-edged hanky in it, a mirror, lipstick, my half-crown ticket and another half-a-crown in case I needed any money apart from my bus fare – sixpence to go and sixpence to return home.

When Peg and I arrived people were already being seated for the dinner. A band was playing a chart-topper of those days – 'Horsey, keep your tail up'. We were very excited as we took our places, looking forward to an evening of dancing and a delicious dinner.

I will now tell you exactly what did happen. The soup (cream of mushroom) was being served. There was a lot of laughter and jolly chat, and as the waiter started to put a plate of soup in front of me, he caught his elbow on the chair-back of the person next to me and ... he tipped the entire portion of soup straight into my lap. It went right through the dress and real silk stockings, and it was very hot. I let out a yell, jumped up, and Peg rushed after me into the Ladies' Room.

Now there's something that isn't as good as it was in 'the good old days' – because it's better – and that's the Ladies' Room. I mean, in those days there were no little piles of hand towels, no machines blowing out hot air, no boxes of paper tissues, nor even soft lavatory paper. All there was was a 'roller-towel' behind the door, already damp with finger marks and so high up we could only reach the bottom two inches, both being little 'uns. And as for drying my dress with it ... impossible.

I had to take the dress off to rinse the soup off the front, disarranging my hair, which was in fashionable 'earphones' – plaits wound round like saucers. I had to get soup off me, as well as the dress, and by now the tears were very near, my cheeks bright red, and the front of my dress dripping wet. We did the best we could with our two little lace-edged hankies, tidied my hair and bravely went back to our dinner places. You will appreciate that by now dinner was nearly over.

Soon the dancing started, and a young fellow came up and asked if he could 'have the pleasure' of this dance. I said, 'I can't dance with a wet frock.' As sharp as a knife he answered, 'I'm not a wet frock!' He said that if we were dancing the wet patch wouldn't show ... and, of course, it didn't. It didn't dry completely, but it did begin to dry and I danced every dance – not always with my new comedian friend, although we danced together quite a lot. By the time the band played 'God Save the King' both Peg and I agreed that we had had a really good half-a-crown's worth.

As I drove by this same Ashton Hall on 5 December, 1990, over fifty years later, with my husband and daughter in a chauffeur-driven limousine ... to be made a Doctor of Literature for Services to Lancashire ... I thought – well, this sort of evens things up, somehow.

So when I stood up at the graduation ceremony to give the reply on behalf of myself and the four other honorary graduates to Princess Alexandra and all the students in the hall who had spent the last three years studying so hard for their degrees – I told them the story of the Lancaster and District Co-operative Annual Dinner and Dance because, in a way, that was how I earned my degree, wasn't it?

20

Morecambe revisited

In 1993 I was awarded the accolade 'Local hero for outstanding achievement as a citizen of Morecambe and Heysham, presented by the *Morecambe Visitor*.' That's the local paper. I'm a 'hero', kindly note, not heroine. I seem to have changed sex.

The pier at Morecambe was a great big chunk of my life, a happy chunk, a marvellous chunk, and talking about it and revisiting it has been part of my life, and also of several television programmes I've made.

One of Russell Harty's shows took me back first. We visited Prompt Corner, Scottie's and my first home together – that's still there. And the clock tower. Now the clock tower at Morecambe, on the promenade, was where we always used to make for to play after school. Your parents would say, 'All right, but be home by five o'clock for your tea.' And you'd have no excuse to be late, you see.

Russell and I were filming near the clock tower, on the Promenade, and believe you me, this was about March, there wasn't a soul, there wasn't even a seagull walking about. There was just us and the film crew.

I said, 'Russell, I used to play round this clock tower

after school.' And I can see Russell now, in his duffel coat, hands in the pockets, looking across at the Central Pier saying, 'That's not the pier that you're always on about, is it?'

Now I have always been so full of pride about the Central Pier, where my father was manager. I promise you the white flagpoles were painted every three months. The flags that fluttered from them, of all nations, were washed and cleaned. It was threepence for a deck chair, and my Dad would say, 'Don't put that one out, it's dirty. No one wants to pay threepence to get their summer dress dirty.' There's a lot of thought in that.

But now, on this dark wet morning, it looked so sad and neglected. Which it was – it was sad and neglected. I said, 'Yes. And if my father could see that now, he'd turn over in his grave, because the pier was ...' and Russell said, 'Well it doesn't look anything now.' I said, 'I'm not asking you to say it looks anything now. I'm asking you to try and imagine – flower boxes all along the edges of the deck, beautiful forms all painted white ...' and I'm standing in the rain, selling him the pier, and he will keep saying 'Yeah, well, it doesn't look like it now.' And in the end I was so cross I said, 'Oh well, you – you've no imagination!' I expected everyone to know the pier as I had known it.

In 1939 the Pavilion on the Pier at Morecambe burned down, and as I've described in the first part of my autobiography, I saw that. There were three domes. They called it the Northern Taj Mahal, because it was the loveliest pavilion of any pier in England. And forgive me telling it again, but round one of the small domes my brother had doves, and round the other dome we grew mustard and cress – a packet of seeds over a damp blanket and it would come up in two days. The day I saw those domes burn down, I stood on the Promenade with hundreds of other people and I thought, 'There's the dovecote gone' – I don't mean the doves were still there – they'd left when my father did, long before. And as the fire crept across, I thought, 'And that's the mustard and cress' – and this was *years* before when we'd done this, when we were kids, but it was all so vivid to me. And the big dome ... but that's all being sad, and this isn't a sad book. But that pier meant so much to me for such a long time. As children we practically lived on it, you see.

In March 1981 the television cameras came back to Morecambe with me for a special *Songs of Praise* in Green Street Methodist Chapel, where year after year my mother had sung the solo 'I Know that My Redeemer Liveth' from Handel's *Messiah*.

It was great to be back. Every time we started filming the introduction in the town, another old friend would come over, saying 'Ee! *Thora*? Is it you?' We'd have a lovely chat, but then we'd have to start the filming all over again from the beginning.

The hymns were accompanied by the local Salvation Army band, the successors of the band I had stood and sang with so often as a child on a Saturday evening, a sixpenny bag of tea-cakes in my hand from Dora's. After tea on a Saturday my mother used to say, 'Go down to Dora's, will you, and get us seven tea-cakes for tomorrow, four currant, three plain – and don't stay too long singing with the Salvation Army.' Because they were always outside Dora's shop on a Saturday, when she did her second baking at six, so you could have your tea-cakes still fresh for Sunday. And Happy Jack, one of the Morecambe fishermen, would be there in his little hat and blue ganzie, his voice so loud they could hear him in Barrow-in-Furness – you could have heard him across the Bay at Grange when he sang 'Onward Christian Soldiers'. That's when that hymn first impressed me so much. He was always called 'Happy Jack', and I don't wonder.

Anyway, for *Songs of Praise* the Salvation Army Band were there, and of course they had their own conductor. But there was another conductor in the pulpit for those of us singing in the congregation. So there were two conductors, do you follow? We all stood up to sing a hymn that is another of my great favourites because it reminds me of my uncles, who were all Morecambe fishermen: 'Will Your Anchor Hold?' 'Our' conductor raised his baton, the Salvation Army band conductor raised his baton ... and suddenly the band was away like an express train: 'Terra-rum-pum-pum-terra-rum-pum-pum ...' and arrived at the end of the first verse and chorus in about twenty seconds flat!

'Our' conductor, the one in the pulpit conducting the congregation, his baton still poised in the air, turned very slowly round and just *looked* at the Salvation Army Band conductor, who, still conducting, turned round too, looking very surprised to see that we hadn't even *started* singing yet! It was quite a comedy routine, and part of a very loving evening of happy memories, laughter and hymn-singing.

I went back quite recently with Melvyn Bragg for *The South Bank Show*, directed by Bryan Izzard, in 1993. But sadly the pier wasn't there by then. When I got back to Morecambe the first thing I did was visit the Promenade, and as I looked I thought, 'Oh! It's gone!' The pier, the piles – everything.

It had looked for years as though it was going to fall down or be washed away. In fact, I remember saying to somebody when I'd been up for a dinner, 'What's going to happen to the pier?' and they had said, 'I think it's been sold to America.' Well, I mean, if you want a joke without a laugh, that's it. So I had said, 'Well, I suggest that they put all the councillors on it, cut it off at this end and let it float to America ... and let it take them with it!' I was always so upset about the pier being neglected, you see, having known what it had been and could be.

So when I was doing *The South Bank Show*, Bryan Izzard filmed me standing on the forebay – all that now remains of the pier – with Scottie, and I chatted to Scottie about when I'd been late for work in my Dad's office, running all the way along the pier. Or, as I used to say, 'up the pier'. My headmistress used to stick her hand up in the air, pointing to the sky and saying 'Thora, the pier does not go up. You either go *on* the pier, or you come *off* the pier.' But I still always said 'up' the pier and 'down' the pier.

I don't know if I ever did a sadder interview, telling Scottie all about it. Saying 'There used to be the ice cream stall ... That's where there used to be the weighing machine, with all the brass polish ... called jockey scales, so you were like half a pound of sausage, you were put on and weighed properly, with weights. And all the lovely automatic machines. Over there was the book kiosk. There was a toffee kiosk. There was Mr Anthony with his little penny cornets. Mr Bradley taking your photograph – a very wet photograph he pinned on your summer dress. Many of those I had taken, for a penny. When I got home there was never anybody on the photograph – it was a grey nothing.'

So that pier, wherever it is, God rest it. It'll be ashes now. It never went to America for its holidays.

Also on *The South Bank Show* we visited the Morecambe Winter Gardens, which at least they are now trying to save – another beautiful place that's been left to fall into disrepair. When I was a kid I used to say to people, because I was a bit of a clever head – 'Did you know that the aerial span of this theatre is bigger than Drury Lane?' I didn't really know what 'aerial span' meant, but I thought it sounded good ... and it was true. It was a wonderful theatre.

For *The South Bank Show* they asked me to stand where the fourth row of the stalls had been. There were little bits of iron, where the seats had been fastened to the floor, and I stood on the fourth row next to the aisle, where I had sat so many years ago the night the Winter Gardens was reopened – beautiful new velvet curtains, everything that could be gilded re-gilded ... but none of that impressed me as much as the drummer in the new sixteen-piece orchestra that had been taken on for the variety shows. I looked at that young drummer and I thought, 'Well, he's not going to get away if I've anything to do with it!' It was Scottie. I stood with him there again, on *The South Bank Show*, and they had put a drumkit in the orchestra pit, where he used to sit. It was a bit sad, in its way.

I'm happy to say that now the Japanese, I think it is, have taken an interest in the Winter Gardens. It's such a beautiful building, and it's just empty, and it really looks so sad. When I was there this last time I was looking at the dress circle and I suddenly remembered the dress circle barmaid, who was always so smart, dressed in black sateen with a corsage on. Barmaids always used to wear a corsage in those days. And all the people who had been top of the bill: Leyton and Johnson, George Formby, Florrie Ford ... great names. I remember Florrie Ford singing 'Has Anybody Here Seen Kelly?' then go off the stage and it was 'three choruses for change' – in theatrical jargon that means that the band played the chorus through three times, and then she came back on in pink sequins, as opposed to blue ones. And a big hat with feathers. Oh, the acts were so beautifully presented.

I know I lived at the right time. I lived at the right time for me, because I have so enjoyed all these things.

21

Postman's Knock

It was in the Winter Gardens' ballroom that my best friend Peg and I had been to a late dance on a Wednesday. It cost a shilling to go, and was open until one o'clock in the morning. We used to buy ten cigarettes – we'd smoke two each on a Wednesday night, and three each on Saturday nights. I say 'we'd smoke' – but really you just sat with your cup of coffee, in the 'fauteuils', a cigarette in your left hand ... we thought it made us look grown up. They were sixpence for ten, and we paid threepence each for a packet a week.

It was coming to the end of this Wednesday night dance; the variety show had been over for two or three hours before that. Peg and I were standing watching the dancing when two gentlemen came and stood near us, and I found I was standing next to Scottie ... I can see him now, in a long black evening overcoat, wearing a white evening scarf with the fringe very near his chin, the other end nearly on the floor, and a black, snap-brimmed trilby. The first thing I thought, when I saw the scarf on lop-sided like that, was 'He's had a drink!' The second thing I thought was, 'What a leading man!' He was medium height, brown hair, very twinkling blue eyes, good cheek bones and he had a dimple in his chin. They started to chat to us, and you could do that in those days, without any fear. Then they offered to see us home, but with such pride I said, 'We have a car.'

We have a car! It was a boy called Edwin Sybil's Austin 7, about as big as a chocolate box, that we used to get about seven of us in. Edwin and his friend, Tollo Bullock, would run us all home. We hadn't spent the evening with them, but we were all part of the same friendly gang. But that evening, as Peg and I went out of the Winter Gardens, down the side steps that lead onto the promenade – we were just in time to see the Austin 7 going whizzing past ... they'd left us behind!

It wasn't far to where I lived, so we started to walk home, and when we were about halfway there, these two 'gentlemen of the orchestra', Scottie and Bill Glover, overtook us and said, 'Have you been stood up?' They walked us home, and that's how I got to know Scottie ... it was really my friend Peg he was interested in, because she was very beautiful.

There were fourteen of us – and when I say 'in a gang', don't misunderstand me. Fourteen of us who were all good friends is what I mean, who visited each other, all our parents knew each other, and each mother would put up once every fourteen weeks with you having all your friends round, and make the sandwiches and whatever else you were having, and we called it a party. I don't suppose the sophisticated young people of today would call it a party – but it was a party.

Well, it was Dorothy Spencer's turn on 14 December, and she had her party, and we were all there, and I went with a boy ... it's awful, but I can't remember who it was. But Peg, my friend, took

Scottie. We had met him and Bill at the dance in about September, and this was a few months later on. It was near enough Christmas to make it a Christmas Party, and all the decorations were up. You used to make your own in those days, with loops of coloured paper.

One of the games we used to play was Postman's Knock – somebody went out of the room, knocked on the door and said 'Post!' and opened the door, and he said who the letter was for, a girl, and she would then go outside with him, the door was shut, he kissed her, then he came back in, and she knocked on the door, called 'Post!' and called a boy out. Very sophisticated, I don't think. But very enjoyable, you see.

On this occasion Peg called Scottie out, and then, really to my surprise, but I suppose it was because I was the only other person he knew there – I can't think of any other reason – Scottie called me out.

And the end of this story is ... we never went back in!

22

A finger of rings

While we were still out of the room for Postman's Knock, Scottie asked me to go with him to the pictures the following night. We went to the Whitehall, and the film had Ronald Coleman and a German actress – I wish I could remember what it was called. And Scottie bought me a box of *Terry's All Gold*. He was to buy me *Terry's All Gold* all my married life – so that's a free advertisement.

Anyone who lives in Morecambe will tell you that when winter gets going there's usually a force-ten gale along the promenade, and there was that night. Opposite the Whitehall was the shelter, for visitors in the summer to sit in, and we just paused in this shelter for me to put my head-scarf on out of the wind. Very politely Scottie said, 'Excuse me, but are you going out with anybody regular?' Lovely expression that, isn't it? I said, 'Well, I've a lot of friends ... but no. Why?' and he said, 'Because if you are, I won't see you again.' What a gent! Anyhow, having said no I wasn't, I saw him every night for four years.

When I say, if I'm giving a talk or anything, that Scottie and I 'were courtin' for three years – some-times, nowadays someone will come up to me after-wards and say, 'What was that word you said, that you and Scottie were?' The first time I didn't know what they were after. I said to this very nice young girl, 'That we were ... very happy?' She said, 'No, it was more like something you did.' She meant 'courting'. She didn't know what courting meant! There are a lot of things, you know, that are going out of the language. I bet half of you reading this book couldn't describe a gas mantle if I asked you ... could you? I think that – not in my lifetime – but by the end of the next century people won't know what all sorts of things were – chimneys, for instance. Do you think young kids will know what chimneys were in fifty years' time?

But back to courting. Now, there were stages of courtship. If you said, 'He's doing a bit of courting' you meant he had his eye on a girl and might be going to ask her out, or might even have taken her out a few times. But if you said, 'He's courting' you meant it was serious – there'd be an engagement ring in about a year.

We got engaged after three years. I've said Scottie was an attractive man, and he was, very good-looking and very charming, and he had been engaged twice before. I never bothered to ask him who broke it off ... the girl or himself.

Anyway, we got engaged, and it was lovely because – I always say 'our' grocer, 'our' greengrocer, they weren't open just for us, but you always called it that – well 'our' jeweller was Jim Hargreaves, whose shop in Euston Road backed on to Cheapside, where we lived, and so of course we went to him for the engagement ring. A lot of time was spent looking at rings on black velvet fingers.

Top As Ivy Unsworth in *In Loving Memory*, with Christopher Beeny as my 'nephew' Billy Henshaw. (© Yorkshire Television)

Above Ready to film *Praise Be!* in the lovely dining room at Mill House. (© BBC)

Top My granddaughter Daisy in the garden at Mill House, with Patch the dog and Quackie, father of all the ducklings. The animals were regular scene stealers during *Praise Be!*. (Courtesy of Janette Scott Rademaekers)

Above A blustery day on location for *Praise Be!* in Goudhurst, Kent, with producer Valetta Stallabrast and crew. (Courtesy of Liz Barr)

My daughter Jan with James and Daisy, when they were both small.
They were all dressed up for a charity fashion show in Beverly Hills –
spot the one whose trousers don't quite fit him! (© Norman I Perle
Photography)

Below This was taken during a happy holiday at Jan's house in Beverly Hills. (© News of the World)

Opposite A proud and memorable day in 1983, when Jan and Scottie came to see me receive my OBE. (© Press Association)

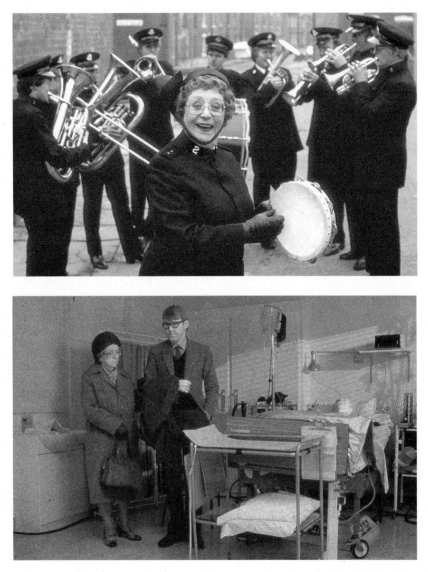

Top As Salvation Army Captain Emily Ridley in *Hallelujah!*. I quite fancied myself in that bonnet! (© Yorkshire Television)

Above Here I am with Alan Bennett, playing his mother in another one of his plays, *Intensive Care*. (© BBC)

That wonderful role in *Cream Cracker Under the Settee*, which did so much for me. I'll always remember how surprised I was at receiving the BAFTA for that – at my time in life! (© BBC)

Left Fancy me becoming a Doctor of Letters of the University of Lancaster! I never could get that velvet cap to sit quite right… (© Lancashire Evening Post)

Below left You've got to laugh when it's as cold and wet as it was that day in Morecambe. Russell Harty and I were filming for one of his shows, in front of Central Pier. (© Lancashire Evening Post)

Below middle Memories of hymns past – it was great to be back for that special *Songs of Praise* filmed in Morecambe, in the very same chapel of my childhood. (© Lancashire Evening Post)

Below right Scottie always did the shopping for us both, bless him, but every now and then I came along.

Opposite I was so thrilled with this beautiful rose, named after me and presented at the Chelsea Flower Show.

Above 'Dame Thora gets her Dameship' … and what a wonderful time we had at Buckingham Palace. James and Daisy flew over specially and darling Scottie gave up his seat so that both grandchildren could be there. (© Press Association)

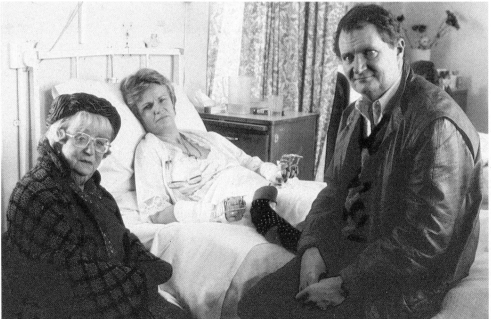

Far left Kathy Staff, Jane Freeman and I in *Last of the Summer Wine*. What fun we have had doing the series over the years! (© BBC)

Below left Julie Walters, Jim Broadbent and I in that sad play *Wide Eyed and Legless*. I played Jim's mother. (© BBC)

Below A beautiful summer's day outside my beloved Jasmine Cottage. (© Peter Jordan, Network Photographers Ltd)

Left A very recent photo of Daisy, all grown up. Doesn't she look lovely?

Below left On pilgrimage in Jordan in 1995, with Rob Marshall, Jan and the tour guide. The desert mountains were the colour of Blackpool rock.

Right This was the opening of a new Stroke Association office in Stafford, where Jan and I unveiled a plaque to Scottie. How nice that it should be there, where he spent so much of his childhood. (© Tony Boydon, courtesy of the Stroke Association)

Below right Here I am telling the Duke of Kent a thing or two, at the 1995 Life After Stroke awards. (© Doug McKenzie, courtesy of the Stroke Association)

Far right My favourite photo of Scottie, with a very young James. This is the picture I say good morning and good night to every day.

Enjoying a good cuppa – one of life's little pleasures! (© Lancashire Evening Post)

I couldn't decide which one I liked best and, knowing us very well, Jim said, 'Take this finger of rings home with you, Thora, and bring it back in the morning.'

He gave us a piece of black velvet with about ten rings on, and we took them home. My mother's face was a study when she saw us put them on the living room table. 'Good gracious!' she said.

'Mr Hargreaves says that Scottie and I can look at them and take our time to decide which one.'

My mother's face! She said, 'You are *not* leaving those here over night.' Now who was going to rob us? I don't know. Number 6 Cheapside, Morecambe, in a street house – we hadn't anything for them to rob. But my mother went to sleep that night with all the rings, on the piece of black velvet, under her pillow. They'd have had to knock her head in to get them!

There was one ring, an African white diamond, not very big, but also not the smallest I've ever seen, I have to say. And each side of it there were three, two and one – tiny, tiny diamonds. The ring was platinum – very modern for those days! It was very pretty, and much the most expensive – about three pounds more than any of the others. I said to Scottie, 'Did either of your other engagements have a bigger ring than that?' and he said, 'No'. So I said, 'Well, I'll have that one then.'

I've still got it, and I always wear it every year on our anniversary, 3 May. I love it. I also had a white gold wedding ring, even though there were certain ladies who said, 'They're not like a *proper* wedding ring, are they?' So I was glad when 'Quackie' Mortimer, a good friend of mine who was getting married at the same time, also chose to have a white gold wedding ring.

I've always loved and treasured both of these rings but, as for many people who marry young, fortunes change and over the years I've been given one or two rather more expensive pieces of jewellery that I'm also fond of, including some rings.

Not so long ago I had a part as an old country woman in an episode of *All Creatures Great and Small* – which I undertook with great joy, may I say. I was up in Yorkshire for the filming, and just as I was coming out of a florist's one morning – because I'd been out to dinner the night before and wanted to send some flowers to my hostess – I came face-to-face with a lady carrying two full plastic bags from the supermarket; these bags were pulling her arms out as she trotted along. She gasped, put down her bags and said, 'Is it Thora?' I said it was, and she said, 'Oh! We always watch you on the telly. We wouldn't miss you for ...' she stopped. She was staring at my hand holding the pot plant I had just bought. '... Where is it?' she demanded. (That was exactly what she said: 'We wouldn't miss you for ...' (pause, change of tone) 'Where is it?')

'Where is what?'

'Your ring! That lovely diamond ring you always wear – like a stamp.'

'Oh, well, I don't always wear it when I come up to film.'

'Oh' she said, 'Don't you? What a shame. I love that ring. I watch you on telly just to look at that ring. Well, ta-ra then.'

And she picked up her two plastic bags and marched off, leaving me standing there feeling quite embarrassed, as if I'd been caught on camera not acting but going 'Have a look at this ring! Eat your hearts out!'

(And may I say to any burglars who may be reading this – it may look like a stamp, but it's nothing like the size of a stamp, it's quite small really, and it was a present from my beloved Scottie and means a lot to me, so please don't steal it!)

23

Scottie and me

Scottie and I were married for fifty-eight wonderfully happy years, and I know just how lucky I've been. It was a marriage, a love affair, a friendship and a partnership. He was better educated than me, and whenever I came across a new word, new to me that is, in a book or newspaper I was reading I would ask him what it meant and how to pronounce it. Then I'd use it as often as I could, bringing it into all our conversations. He was very good, but many's the time he'd say to me, 'Would you like to find another new word to use? You've been using that last one in all the wrong places for a fortnight, and I'm getting a bit tired of it now!'

When I first started jotting down little thoughts into an exercise book, ideas of things to put in this book, Scottie was with me, and I'd like to include some of them in this chapter, just as I originally wrote them when he was pottering around in the garden outside, or sitting in his favourite armchair next to me. I hope it will give you something of the flavour of our everyday life together, Scottie and me.

DECEMBER 1993

It's amazing the things you can put into books these days, that you couldn't at one time. I mean, I don't mind telling you now that I was a virgin when I got married. I'm not swanking about it – I was. I must admit that sometimes when Scottie and I are having a laugh – and, bear in mind, my husband is a good-looking man who always has a twinkle in his eye for a pretty girl, and the thing is most women have a twinkle in their eye for him, too! – I say to him, just for fun, 'You know, if I had my life over again, I wouldn't be a virgin when I got married.'

And he'll say, 'Oh yes you would!'

'Oh no I wouldn't! ... I think probably, I would have liked to have had the experience of ten men ...'

'Don't be daft!'

'All right ... twelve men, then!'

It was a different world when we were young, and I married him in white. There was a character, Bella, I played many times in the forties and fifties in productions of *Saturday Night at the Crown*, the play that Walter Greenwood wrote especially for me. Old Bella has a few stouts inside her, and she says to the two men at the next table in the pub, talking about a girl who's just left, 'And I'll tell you something else – thems falsies she's wearing ... Talks about getting married in white? God forgive her!'

It used to bring the house down. I suppose there

are young people today who wouldn't even know what that line meant, would they?

JANUARY 1994

Scottie was up at 4.30 this morning, and I joined him for a cuppa in the lounge at 5.30. We love the first few hours that start our day. Not that we're always drinking tea at 5.30 am – but I would say that eight mornings out of ten we are. Breakfast is always the same – lovely hot buttered wholemeal toast, spread with Marmite for me and home-made marmalade for Scottie.

We always – well, nearly always – watch the six o'clock news in the mornings. Of course I often have to be up at that hour anyway, because a car will be coming to pick me up at 6.15 to take me off to work, when I'm filming out of London. I've often been swept off at 5.30 if the filming is quite a distance away. I love a busy life!

15 FEBRUARY, 1994:
PANCAKE TUESDAY

Full marks! Well done! Credit where it's due ... and all that jazz. It is a well-known fact – or should be – that Scottie makes pancakes better than anyone in the world. I mean it! They're splendiferous ... and I've just eaten *five* ... so I should know! Hot and sizzling from the pan, with fine sugar sprinkled on them and fresh lemon juice squeezed over the sugar. Ooh, blimey! Even writing about it makes my mouth water – I wonder if there are any more? Excuse me a moment.

Do you know, he's made pancakes on Shrove

Tuesday every year of our marriage apart from the six years during the War when he was in the airforce? Honestly, he seems to improve yearly. It's been a wonderful week for grub. On Monday we had every sort of vegetable nearly, diced into small cubes – onions, celery, carrots, turnips, peas, corn and potatoes mixed with cubes of shin beef all in gravy.

THURSDAY 17 MARCH, 1994: ST PATRICK'S DAY

It's amazing how many people ask me, 'Do you enjoy your work?'

I can honestly answer 'Yes I do,' but what I'm going to say now is not about enjoying 'the acting bit', it's about duties – yes, duties – that I enjoy when playing my housewife character – I mean, that is, being me, myself, at home with Scottie.

I'm sure a lot of you will agree that there are a lot of household tasks you simply hate doing, whilst there are others you enjoy. I know someone who enjoys making beds; I have another friend who would happily spend her life cleaning and dusting. I even know someone who likes ironing! Everyone's different, aren't they?

Well me, meself, personally (as my old dresser used to say), I dislike ironing and making beds (so I'm glad I'm not a chambermaid!). However, I like the effect of these jobs, so I always make my bed as soon as I get up and before I go to the bathroom, so that when I return from my ablutions I gaze on a neatly made bed, with my lovely white tri-pillows sitting at the top.

In case you are just about dropping off at this
point, I shall now tell you all about one job I *love*
… when I'm at home at that time of day, that is …
here it comes: making our tea! Now then, isn't
that exciting? Wasn't that worth staying awake
for?

I love the two of us being in the kitchen together,
the smell of tea being brewed, of wholemeal
bread being toasted and buttered, making the
sandwiches, perhaps with tuna emptied into a
bowl with some finely chopped onion, a dessertspoon of tomato puree, a dessertspoon of salad
cream or mayonnaise, a suggestion of salt and
pepper, a splash of vinegar … mix all together
then, using a spatula, spread it over the buttered
bread. Should you also want a slice of lettuce or
some watercress, lightly salted, in the sandwich –
add it! Scrumptious.

Hold on, though, here's another tasty little offering coming up. We always have a jar of sliced
onion in vinegar in our sauce cupboard. Do you?
Did you notice that bit? Sauce Cupboard? Ahem!
Well, we need one, don't we? For all the sauces,
spices and herbs we use. For this next little item,
toast some bread lightly under the grill, take it
out and spread the untoasted side with butter or
marge or whatever you use, then carefully
arrange some sliced onion on each piece and
cover that with slithers of cheese (preferably
strong, crumbly Lancashire farmhouse, if you can
get it). Pop it all back under the grill until the
cheese is melted and golden. Sprinkle a little
Worcester sauce on it before eating – or, and this

is me, soy sauce. I cannot describe the sensation of the first mouthful – except to say that it is bloomin' splendiferous.

I know this isn't a cookery book, but I'll just add another sandwich filling, which is one of our own originals: you need a tin of corned beef, an onion, three fresh tomatoes, salt and pepper. Pour boiling water over the tomatoes and leave for one minute, then you can easily remove the skins. Put all the ingredients through the mincer until it's like a paste. Result? Indescribably tasty sandwich spread. It is, honestly ... do try it. We always have dishes of sandwiches with this filling when we give parties, and they always go first, there is never one left, and everybody asks how to make the filling.

If – and I do mean *if* – you are still hungry after that, have a portion of pears (Conference), lightly stewed in water with a dash of brandy, cloves and brown sugar. All prepared by Chef Scottie the day before. Ooh, mate! Finish up with two or three cups of Earl Grey tea in your favourite armchair.

And I hereby declare that our 'tea-time revels', either in London or in our country kitchen, are the favourite 'part' of my life.

Of course, I don't know if I'd enjoy it so much if it wasn't Scottie who was the other character in these particular performances!

Looking back at these diaries has a bit of sadness about it, now that these things can only be memories. But no one who has been loved as much as I was for as

long as I was – fifty-eight wonderfully happy years –
has any right to feel sorry for themselves. So I won't
be. I'll just say 'Thank you, Scottie – I loved every
minute of it.'

24

Shhh – Can you keep a secret?

I don't want to boast about doing things well, but I will boast about one thing, and that is, I can keep a secret. I can keep a secret *very* well ... An example of just how good I am, just to show you, goes back to when I was at school. One day one of my friends, Connie, said to me, 'Can you keep a secret?' and I said, 'Oh yes!' and we locked little fingers on it. (People of my age reading this book might know that locking your little fingers, that means 'I Promise.') Connie told me something which I never told anyone – nothing would have dragged it out of me.

I ran into her again – oh, *years* later, I suppose we would both have been in our fifties by then – and I said, 'You know that secret you told me while we were at school? I've never told *anybody!*' And she said, 'What secret?' And I said to her, 'Oh, Connie! You remember! One afternoon you told me such a secret, and we locked little fingers on it, and you said, "You won't tell anybody, will you?" And I said, "No I won't" and I can tell you now, I never have told a soul.'

She started laughing and said, 'Well can you tell *me*? I've forgotten what it was!' And I said, 'Your periods had started! You said, "Promise me you won't tell anybody" and honestly, I never have!' And she said, 'Well, you can now – I've just gone through the change!'

So now I've told you – but believe me, you would never have heard it from my lips before now!

25

Let's have the Irish jig!

Prior to having a heart by-pass operation in 1992 I had a ... I wish I could remember the long word for what they were going to do, but any of you who have experienced it will know that they put wires along your veins, with a little sort of balloon thing on the top, and if the balloon blows up, that vein's all right. That's as near as I can tell you.

There was a little room with six little beds in it, and there were four gentlemen and a lady and myself all waiting for ... whatever this examination was. When it was my turn I was called through into the little operating theatre, and there were three or four nurses standing there, and the first thing they said when I went in was, 'Do you like Ella Fitzgerald, Mrs Scott?'

I must admit I thought, 'What a peculiar thing to ask me,' but I said, 'Oh, yes ... yes. She's very clever.' I suppose I must have had rather a strange expression, and one of the nurses said, 'Only, you see, we've only got three tapes, and Doctor – WhateverHisNameWas – likes to do this to music.'

So I said, 'I see. Well – what are the other two?' She looked and said, 'Well, er, this one's an Irish jig ...' I said, 'That'll do! Let's have the Irish jig.'

So I lay there, with these wires being pushed

through, to the strains of this Irish jig 'De, la de li da de do da, blero, dub dub dub ...' because I'm a great admirer of Irish dancing and the tunes. And the doctor carried on with his work, very seriously ...

I went back into the other room and in about five minutes the doctor came through and said, 'I think an operation, don't you?' And I said, 'Well, I don't know. You're here to tell me that.' And he said, 'Yes. We'll say the 26th of January.'

There's nothing funny about the operation, when it's open-heart surgery. In fact the only thing to smile about is I've felt so much better since. It was such a success, I might even be able to manage a bit of an Irish jig myself!

26

Incredible illucinations

Have you ever experienced an hallucination? Because if you haven't ... don't bother. In fact, a lot of what I'm going to tell you isn't very nice, so if you're easily upset, miss out this chapter.

Just after my open-heart surgery, while still at St Mary's Hospital, I suffered from hallucinations – and I'm here to tell you, they were not at all funny.

I said to Jan, 'What are all those little chickens with red caps on doing under that sink?' And she said, 'What chickens? Which sink?' There were *thousands* of them. Tiny little chickens, red combs. In the end, Jan couldn't convince me, so she said, 'I'll go and pick some up and bring them for you.' She came back and said, 'There's nothing there, Mummy.' I said, 'Well, there's some pigeons there, with cooks' hats on.'

Then I thought the room was a foot deep in flour. I said to Scottie, 'Oh look! It's all over the knees of your suit and everything!' He said, 'What is?' I said, 'This flour.' He said, 'Which flour?' I said, 'All over the floor!' He said, 'There isn't any flour!'

I said, 'What? You're going to tell me in a minute there aren't two miniature polo bears standing up there!' He said, 'Well, there aren't.' I said, 'There *are* – they're only as big as guinea pigs.'

I was in Liberty's in Regent Street, two o'clock in the morning, everything was pink, the counters and everything. Jan was with me, covered in a pink sheet. I went out into Regent Street. There was a clock. A quarter to two, it said. Nobody there, and I came back and said to her, 'There's nobody in Regent Street.' She said, 'No, there won't be ... What are you doing?' And I said, 'I've lost my See-No Net.'

That was after the heart by-pass. Then with the last operation that I had, in 1994, on my leg, I was out for four hours. And Jan *told* the surgeons, in front of me, 'I don't know whether there are new drugs these days, but two years ago my mother nearly drove this hospital mad with hallucinations.' They said, 'Oh, she'll have a few.' I did as well. It's the anaesthetic.

Thank God Jan was always there the following morning, because I had terrible dreams. She slept in a chair by my bed. Every morning I would say 'Did I?' or 'Didn't I?' or 'Did we or did we not?' I said to her one day, 'Did we sleep on the stage of the Grand Theatre in Blackpool last night?' and she said, 'No, Mummy, of course we didn't.' I said, 'Oh, come off it! There was a three-piece suite that was used in the play, and I got in one of the chairs, and didn't a woman of the streets come up and give me two tablets in a glass? And I wouldn't take them?' She said, 'No. No. Oh dear, here we go again!'

There were lots of mornings like that. Then there was a lady doctor, who came and took my blood-pressure, and as she went away I noticed that on the floor she'd dropped a half-hoop of five-pound notes, sprayed out evenly, and three twenty-pound notes folded up. So I waited until another doctor, a young man, came into the room, and I said, 'Oh, do excuse me, you know the doctor that just went out? She's just dropped those on the floor.' And he said, 'Dropped what?' I said, 'The five-pound notes – there, on the floor.' He said, 'I can't see any five-pound notes.' I said, 'Oh come along! Don't be stupid! There's a whole arc of five-pound notes, and three twenty-pound notes ... I'm looking at them now – folded ... and that lady has just been in, because these two gentlemen ...' and I turned round and the two men who were sitting there had no heads ... and the doctor said, 'Well, Mrs Scott, it's all right, but there aren't any five-pound notes.'

The thing that gives me the most horrible feeling of fear is that there will be a black beetle or a cockroach. I've never been able to stand them. So when they moved me to a room further along the corridor, I sat in a chair, looked down, and there were four beetles. I called for the nurse. I said, 'I'm so sorry to trouble you, but I can't stick beetles, and look, there's four there ...' And she said, 'Where?' 'There ...' She said, 'I can't see any beetles.' I said, 'Oh look, they're *moving*. Of course you can!' So she went and got a mop out of a wet mop bucket, slopped it on them, and went off. And I sat there. I cannot explain how I feel when I see a beetle. And I saw three more, in front of me. So I called her again. She said, 'What is it now?' I said, 'There's three more beetles – there ... there.' She said, '*Where?*' I said, '*There, look!* Walking on the floor.' So she goes for the mop again. Slops it.

I'm sitting in this chair, not knowing what to do in case I see another beetle, and a girl who must have been Flower Power, covered in flowers and everything, was asleep on my right, with a very well-dressed man with her. And I said, 'Did you see those beetles?' And he shook his head, and I thought, 'I'm not sticking this! I'm not sitting here in this chair in this dark room with beetles crawling all over!' And I went outside and got in a car. I said, 'Would you take me home, please?' And a friend took me home to where I was born, in Cheapside.

The following morning I said to Jan, 'I must set about ordering a 'phone for my mother.' And she said, 'Why, Mummy?' And I said, 'Because I noticed, when I went home last night, she'd wondered where I'd been, and she's not on the 'phone.' Jan had quite a bit of trouble persuading me that my mother had been dead for years.

Apparently I was in the same room all the time, from going in to coming out. I was never taken to another room. I thought there was another bed next to mine with a white-haired, very nice old gentleman in it, and a lady of about seventy with a nice perm. There was a television at the bottom of their bed, and when it got to one o'clock I said to the nurse, 'Would they mind if I had the news on?' So whether she asked them or not I don't know. Anyhow, later on in the afternoon Jan arrived, and the television was on the floor on its side. I said, 'Did somebody knock that television over or something?' And the nurse said, 'Which television?' I said, 'That one, at the bottom of their be ...' And there was no bed! Nobody in it. And I said, 'Just excuse me, will you? There was an old lady and gentleman in a bed here this morning, wasn't there?' She said, 'No. There's only been your bed in here.' And I said to Jan, 'Take no notice!

There was a man and a woman in bed here, with a television ...'

Jan said the best one was when the surgeons came in one day, and they said, 'How are you, Mrs Scott?' Jan herself had been out of the room going to the loo or something, and they'd walked in with her and they'd been talking, and I said, 'Very well thank you.' And Jan said, 'Well, I'm afraid Mummy's had a few hallucinations.' And I said, 'Nothing that matters, you know.' And they went out, and I said to Jan, 'You can tell those people to come out from behind the television now!'

I think I was quite a disruption to the life of the hospital, but Jan says I wasn't, because there was only her with me all the time.

Now, what is there prettier and nicer to talk about ...?

27

A hen called 'Thora'

I went to the Chelsea Flower Show in 1988, and as I approached the Rosemary Roses stand the press cameras were clicking away. Rosemary Roses had written to me the year before to ask if they could 'bred' – which is the funny word they use – and name a rose after me, and of course I had said they could – who wouldn't be proud and honoured to have a rose named after them? All the roses on the stand were breathtaking, and there in the middle was a very large display of the palest of pink roses, almost white, with hair-fine lines of deep pink and the most wonderful perfume. I felt like crying ... the name-ticket on them said 'Thora Hird'.

It's a floribunda rose or, as Jan always calls it, a 'Thorabunda' ... to think that years after I've gone to live in 'the great entertainment world in the sky' such a beautiful rose with my name will still be growing in people's gardens and giving pleasure.

Actually, I've got quite a collection of living things named after me now.

Many of them have come as a direct result of working on *Praise Be!* Liz Barr, the original producer of *Praise Be!*, still went on writing the *Praise Be!* scripts with me after she left the BBC, and if ever you saw me visiting a place to interview someone where there would be animals in the picture, you can be sure it was at Liz's suggestion, because she is someone who, like my daughter Jan, is daft about animals.

For instance, in 1993 I went to talk to Paul Heiney on his traditional Suffolk farm. Oh – magic is the only word for it. He had all the old farming equipment, shire horses to do the ploughing, and a shepherd's hut on wheels to take into the fields during lambing, and a farmyard full of hens, sheep and pigs – all just as I remember farms from when I was a child. It was like travelling back to another age. I'll never forget sitting with Paul on a hay bale in the evening sun, surounded by the sounds and smells of the farm, talking about faith. And after my visit, when his big black sow Alice had a litter, he wrote in his column in *The Times* – I've still got the cutting – that because he'd so enjoyed my visit, and because he was sure I wouldn't mind, he was naming one of the piglets 'Thora' in my honour. Well, I thought it was indeed an honour!

Another year I visited the Donkey Sanctuary in Sidmouth, in Devon, to interview the founder Elizabeth Svendsen, MBE. Dr Svendsen founded the Sanctuary to take in unwanted and ill-treated donkeys and give them a home for life. Today there are over six thousand donkeys living there, and the Sanctuary needs a computer to keep all the details. But every single donkey is treated as an individual. Some of them go on to earn their keep once they are well and strong enough, by giving rides to little disabled children. For these children, making friends with such gentle, friendly creatures, and riding on them, gives them self-confidence in all sorts of ways, and it can be an important part of their development.

I've always loved donkeys. Donkey rides were part of the seaside holiday for both children and grown-ups when I was growing up in Morecambe ... All these years later I can still recall the sound of the donkeys going home each summer evening after their hard day's work on the sands – the harness, with its bells on the brow-bands, jingling as their big heads nodded up and down, their little hooves tapping along the sea-washed stones of the ramparts. We children would run along beside them for a few yards, patting their hindquarters, and as we called out 'Goodnight, Neddy!' they would blink their heavy-lashed eyelids, as much as to say 'Goodnight, children, we'll be back tomorrow.'

All my life I have wanted to ride through the coun-tryside – not on the stage, I mean, like at the London Palladium, but properly, along country lanes – in a little donkey-cart. And I did it there, at the Donkey Sanctuary, in my 79th year – and I have to tell you, I enjoyed it more than if they'd given me a mink coat or a cottage with a thatched roof! It was another dream come true.

The other thing that was lovely was that one of the donkeys in the Sanctuary had been expecting a foal the night before I arrived, and they said, 'If it's a girl, we'll call it Thora, because she's coming tomorrow.' Well, it wasn't, it was a boy, so they called it Thor, which is just as flattering, because all my closest friends call me Thor.

But I've another one! I had the joy of visiting a convent, All Hallows, Ditchingham, in Norfolk. Now

I don't know, why do we always think that a Mother Superior will be an elderly nun with a kindly round face and called Martha? The Mother Superior at All Hallows is called Sister Pamela. You wouldn't think of a Mother Superior as 'Pamela', would you? Well I wouldn't, although I don't know why, really.

I don't know how to describe her. She is the most wonderful person, attractive, clever and kind, the most loving, dear person that I'll ever meet.

I had a happy day filming there – animals everywhere, and such a warm, loving atmosphere, I wish I could describe it better. In the kitchen, where they were washing up, there was a cat sitting on the windowsill, watching them.

It's where Sister Maud lived, who, between the ages of eighty and ninety, wrote a collection of little poems called 'Tailwags'. The sisters collected them together in a little book, and before I ever went to the convent I had been quoting Sister Maud on *Praise Be!* Here's an example:

> *'Only the tail-end of life is left,' I said,*
> *And into my head*
> *A thought came out of the blue,*
> *A thought from you:*
> *'But that is the cheery end,' you said,*
> *'So see*
> *That you use it for me.'*
> *And I said 'Amen' and raised my head.*
> *'I will glorify God with a wag,' I said!*

While I was there it was time to feed the hens. And there was one sister, a girl of about twenty-three, plump, beautiful, smiling face, black waist apron on. She took me to see the hens being fed, and on the way she said, 'By the way, you'll see a hen in a minute that lays blue eggs!' Well, you're not going to say 'Are you telling the truth?' to a nun, so I said, 'Does it?' And she said, 'Yes, and not the blue of a thrush's egg. Bluer than that!'

And there, indeed, were four beautiful *blue* eggs. It was a black hen. She said, 'We thought we'd like to call it Thora ... Would you be offended?' Offended? It was the proudest day of my life!

At the end of that day's filming at Ditchingham something quite strange happened. Not that what happened at the end of the day was strange, I don't mean that, but just listen. Or 'read on', I should say.

We were travelling in a large hired car, and as we were leaving I got in the front and Chris Mann, the very clever director of *Praise Be!* that year, got in the back, leaned over and slammed my front door shut – just as Sister Pamela leaned in to kiss me goodbye ... and these dear little fingers on this dear little hand were caught ... Oh, I *felt* it. I was so upset. And I looked at her, and I knew she was fighting for the tears not to come, and she said, 'Oh, I ... ah ... I ...' I was out of that car quicker than I've told you, and I put my arms round her and said, 'Oh! Your little hands!' She said, 'I'll go and put them under water.' Which she did, and we had to leave her and drive off. I hated that journey, thinking about her ... and I didn't speak to poor Chris the whole way back! I know he didn't mean it, but it really had upset me.

That night the whole crew of us stayed at a motel. I've never been as cold in my life! I'll tell you, I woke up in the middle of the night, opened my case and put on three cardigans, wrapping one round my legs – you should have seen me! Well, you shouldn't have seen me. Thank goodness you didn't see me.

This was, I'd say, about three o'clock, half past three in the morning, because I looked at my watch and I thought, 'Good gracious me, I've got to freeze for another five hours!' And then I wakened again at half past six, still very cold. But when I wakened both times, my first thought was for these little fingers, and each time I said a little prayer for her. I said, 'Dear God, please don't let her hands be injured or maimed.'

During the following day I tried to get her twice on the telephone. Both times they were at prayer, so I didn't worry again. But the following day I got her on the telephone, and I said, 'I'm just ringing up to see about your poor fingers,' and she laughed and said, 'We-ell! My nails are going a little bit purple and blue, but they are all right and I'm not in pain. By the way ...' she said, 'Did you say prayers for me that night?' And I said, 'Yes, I did.' She said, 'Yes, I knew. What time? Was it about half past three?' I said, 'Well, round about then! And then again ...' and we both said together, '... at about half past six.'

I said to her, 'Well, how would you know?' She said, 'I didn't know for sure, but I did feel you were praying for me.'

We've kept in touch by letter ever since. She always ends her letters with a P.S. 'Love from the hen!' They're having a new bit built on to the side of the convent, where you can go if you've been ill, and I've said that whatever else I'm doing, I'll be along to open that. I had a letter from Pamela the other day, while I was writing this chapter. She wrote:

A few weeks ago I had a lovely, restful holiday with some friends who live on a farm near Kingston. They keep Welsh black cattle. While I was there a lot of lovely little calves were born, and I told my friends about Thora the Hen, so now there is also a delightful frisky Welsh black calf called Thora!'

So you see, that's a rose, a pig, a donkey, a hen that lays blue eggs, and now a Welsh black calf – all called Thora! And it's not bad going, is it? You'd have to go more than a day's march, wouldn't you, to meet somebody else who had all that?

28

All things bright and beautiful

My mother loved the simple flowers that grow on the railway side, marguerites, dog daisies, foxgloves and – I think above all – cowslips. I was speaking at a lunch, and amongst the gentlemen of the press there was Keith Waterhouse, a clever writer, a northerner, and we were chatting and I said, 'I can remember something you wrote – eight or nine years ago. I remember it vividly' and he said, 'Gracious! Was it so inspiring?' I said, 'Well, it was because you mentioned cowslips. You said there aren't as many cowslips these days. And I remember turning to Scottie and saying, "He's right!"'

He *was* right. When I was a child, if you went along any railway side, or in my case along the canal bank, you could always pick a bunch of cowslips. I thought about Keith Waterhouse's article so much, and the next time I was in a garden centre I was roaming through and I saw there were some cowslips, so I bought a pot, thinking I would give them love and care as never. And you think I'm going to say, 'And now there's a huge bed of cowslips', don't you? But there isn't. I could do nothing with them. I used to talk to them and say, 'Aren't you feeling so well, loves? Shall I take you indoors?' But they did nothing.

Nothing. Which is rare for me, because I'm not clever but there isn't much that doesn't come up once I've planted it.

I've got those books of gardening by the Old Wives, which say things like, 'If you're going to cut down an elm tree, don't do it until the third Thursday in the month, and face the south.' They may be right! One thing they say that I have proved does work very well: 'If your roses are covered with green fly, get a piece of garlic and plant a small bulb underneath each rose bush.' I can't stand garlic in food, it always upsets me, but we grow lots of roses, so I tried this. With a dibber I put a little bulb of garlic underneath each rose bush. And you're going to say, 'And the roses were still all covered in green fly ...' Well, they weren't. We didn't have a green fly all summer on the roses. Apparently they are like me – garlic upsets them.

I can be absolutely mesmerised when I'm gardening. Take Gypsophilia seed – it's like powder. Whenever I'm planting seeds I'm thinking, 'This little bit of dust is going to turn into a bush full of little white flowers ...'

Scottie so often used to find me standing transfixed in the garden, staring at seeds in my hand, and he'd say, 'Oh, hallo! Are we off again – meditating?' and I'd say, 'Yes, we are, because I cannot believe that this little, tiny, mite of thing is going to be a bed of snapdragons!'

Autumn and winter can be breathtaking too, can't they? The changing colours of the leaves on the trees, spiders' webs along the hedges, silver with dew, and the aroma of garden rubbish being burned on bonfires.

Oh, I love that! And the end of the year, with the sparkling frost outlining every leaf and branch and blade of grass, until we reach that magic moment when the year turns, and the first dear little snowdrop pushes its way into view.

I've always admitted we're a bit daft in our family – regarding certain things, that is. And snowdrops – or at least the arrival of same – has always meant a great deal to us. When Jan lived in Beverly Hills I would always keep my eyes open in January for the first bunch of snowdrops to appear in London on the barrows. I would buy a bunch and put them in a certain china vase that had belonged to Jan and which she had loved when she was a little girl. Then I'd ring Beverly Hills, whatever time of day it was, and say 'Hey, Jan! I've just put some snowdrops in your little vase.' It always delighted her. Not exactly an earth-shaking event, I know, but the sort of thing our family's life has been full of and blessed by.

Of course, now that Jan and William live in Sussex they have patches of snowdrops all over their garden each year, and I have some in my cottage garden, too. And do you know – yes, of course you do – if I am in London when the first little white treasure pops through, Jan will ring up and say 'Guess what!' and I will say, 'A snowdrop is out!' Not very sophisticated, are we?

I think I told you all this about the snowdrops in my last book – so if I did, I apologise that you've had to pay twice to read the same thing.

This is only a 'little' story, but it is so full of love that I want to tell it to you. It holds love, sadness and great joy ... that's why I'm telling you. I would like to begin 'Once upon a time ...' but that would be silly, and this is not a fairy story, but a true one.

You remember I've told you about the mallard ducks in Jan's garden at Isfield? Well, one year, when Mother Mallard's twelve little ducklings were just old enough to go on the lake in the Millhouse grounds, we all watched them swimming about with as much admiration and oohing and ahing as though no ducklings had ever swum on a lake before. When Mother Mallard came off the water and waddled off, the dutiful babies followed her in a fluffy yellow line ... beautiful ... But suddenly Jan said, 'Hey! Hold on a minute. There's one missing ...' Needless to say, we all started counting aloud 'One, two, three ...' but at eleven we each stopped. We all started to search among the reeds and plants growing around the lake, but no luck. Isn't it amazing how quickly joy can turn to sorrow? Only a few minutes before we had been enthusing about the little duck family swimming about, and now suddenly ... misery and anxiety. Mother Mallard sat down after shaking her feathers, and her family pecked at the grass and quite honestly showed not the slightest concern that one of them was missing.

Oh, hecky plonk! It was going to be a very upsetting evening for Scottie, William, Jan and me. The dogs had been with us when we were watching the display on the lake, but then had wandered off somewhere. Just as we were giving up searching for the missing duckling, Jan saw Patch trotting towards us from the far end of the lawn. Jan gave a little gasp, and then gently said, 'Come here, Patch.' As Patch approached we all saw the head of the tiny mallard duckling hanging out of her mouth. That was all. Just the head. 'Patch, come here' Jan said again. She was kneeling down. Patch approached and sat down in front of her. Jan put her hand out palm upwards, and Patch dropped the baby duckling onto Jan's hand. We held our breaths. The duckling stood up. Shook itself. Hopped off Jan's hand, down onto the grass, and joined its brothers and sisters! There was nothing wrong with it!

Patch, bless her, had realised the little thing had wandered away from the rest of the family, picked it up in her soft 'gun-dog' mouth, and returned the happy wanderer to Jan. Praises, pats, biscuits were showered on 'You wonderful dog! Who's a good girl, then?' and Patch just sat there, laughing, because dogs do laugh you know. Her face seemed to be saying, 'I bet you dozy lot thought I'd eaten that duckling, didn't you?' Well, let's be honest, we dozy lot *had* thought that!

You've heard of the 'happy hour' haven't you? It's usually in a pub, when the drinks are cheaper for an hour, but I'm not referring to that kind of 'happy hour' – I'm referring to a *very* happy hour I have just experienced.

I needed some eggs, and Jan said she would run me down the lane to Boathouse Farm. I said, 'Give me ten minutes to get myself ready.'

'You don't need to bother too much,' she said, 'You'll only be meeting cows and sheep!'

She was right ... but not quite. We *did* see cows and sheep at Boathouse Farm, but we saw something else – dozens of 'em, all beautiful – lambs and calves. I'm not exaggerating, honestly, I have never ever seen such wonderful offspring, and some of the lambs had been born only the previous night, and some that very morning. They were all frisking about, and a tiny, dark grey, black-legged one ran straight up to me. I picked it up and stroked its tiny nose with my little finger. It put its little mouth round my finger and started to suck like mad. I apologised to it, and told it the Milk Bar wasn't open. I looked down and there was Mum, who had walked over and was baaing something, perhaps it was, 'Now I've told you not to talk to strangers!'

Jan was cuddling a dear little white lamb, quite content to snuggle against Jan's warm heart. The farmer's wife, Mrs Martin, is such a kind person, and she amazed me by telling me something about every individual sheep and lamb, things like, 'That lamb won't feed off its mother, so we're bottle feeding it' or, 'You see that mother over there? She had triplets ...' and so on. Not only did the mother sheep all look exactly alike to me, so did the lambs, apart from being black or white. But to Mrs Martin they were all unique individuals.

There was a little grey-and-black lamb in a pen on its own, and Mrs Martin said, 'That one's an orphan.' Now until she said the word 'orphan' I had been thinking how happy and contented it looked. But an orphan! I suddenly felt very sad and the tears started to well up. But Mrs Martin said very cheerfully, 'It'll be all right. One of the girls from the village is coming for it, and she'll hand-rear it.'

We moved into the cowsheds, where there were dozens of very large cows, all lying down, chewing the cud. The building smelled of fresh hay, and I've never experienced such serenity except in a convent or church. The animals looked so content, and a few had little calves cuddled up beside them. One calf was just a few hours old, and looked at Jan and me with its sweet little face on one side, as much as to say, 'So this is the great big world, is it?'

Oh, I did enjoy that afternoon. I was sad to leave them all.

All the way home I was singing the words of one of my favourite hymns, 'All Things Bright and Beautiful', and especially the chorus:

> *All things bright and beautiful*
> *all creatures great and small*
> *all things wise and wonderful*
> *– the Lord God made them all.*

29

Nothing like a Dame

Of course, in all our lives we have exciting moments. I had an extra-wonderful moment when a letter arrived from Downing Street to say I was to be awarded the OBE. I had to watch it, because you can lose your OBE if you tell anybody. You can! You can lose that OBE by going into your grocer's next day and saying, 'Hey! Do you know, I'm getting the OBE!' Until the official announcement it is strictly private.

Nobody was more surprised than I was when I got it, although at first I supposed that OBE must mean Outside Broadcasting Expert! You are always given the full title if you are speaking at a nice luncheon, when they'll say, 'And our speaker is Miss Thora Hird, Most Excellent Order of the British Empire', that's what it is, and it sounds even better.

You see, I think I get so much more pleasure out of achievements like this, because I wasn't always *it*, if you know what I mean. Thora Hird, OBE ... scrubbed her mother's steps ... didn't know what the word 'arse' meant!

In September 1992 we'd been on a cruise, Scottie and I, and when we got back, as always, we couldn't open the front door for the mail. We had a routine: put them in piles: Thora Hird, Mr James Scott, T. and J. Scott Ltd, and then we opened them accordingly. One Thora Hird envelope looked a bit important so I opened it, to read a very nice letter informing me that I was to be made a Dame of the Most Excellent Order of the British Empire.

Well you can imagine how I felt, can't you? Here it was, in print, on 10 Downing Street notepaper. As before, when the recipient receives the news, they are requested, nay, ordered (politely) to tell NO ONE. It can be very difficult, let me tell you. For one thing, my husband was reading my letter over my shoulder. But I can swear on my life that we told no one, not even Jan.

People don't seem to think of me the same way as I think of myself. Even after I'd got the OBE people would still say to me, 'Why haven't you been made a Dame?!' and even, '*When* are they going to make you a Dame?' It's not that I want to swank about this, but it's just that I find it so moving, and so strange – there was even one man in Brighton who wrote every week of his life, until I got it. They must have said in the end, 'Oh, it's that man again! Give it 'er! Give it 'er, because we're getting fed up of all this!'

When I telephoned Downing Street – to make sure it was right, because, as I told them, 'I've already got the OBE' – they said it was right.

In June 1993 I was making a series of programmes for the BBC, produced and directed by Bryan Izzard, called *Thora on the Broad and Narrow* at Pinewood Studios. I couldn't tell you how many films I made at Pinewood for Rank Films before the war. I don't mean I starred in any of them – they were mostly one-day, two-day character parts. But it was like a homecoming, and when I was back there doing *Thora on the Broad and Narrow*, almost every day there would be rat-a-tat on my dressing room door and someone would stick their face round and say 'Hallo, Thora, do you remember me?'

On the day the Honours list was announced – 11 June, 1993 – I was sitting in my dressing room at lunchtime, not aware that at that very moment the list was being read out on the one o'clock news. I had had an early call that morning and hadn't seen the papers or spoken to anybody, and I honestly didn't remember that that was the day the list was to be published.

There was a knock on my door and a very happy looking floor manager came in saying, 'Who keeps things very quiet, Thora?' I answered 'Who ... what? What are you talking about?' He then said, 'Will you please come on the set – *Dame* Thora.'

I went along with him, and as I entered the set the music of 'There is nothing like a Dame ...' was playing, and the champagne corks started popping. Everyone was very kind, bless 'em, and it was lovely that it happened when I was there, at Pinewood, a place so full of memories for me.

When I returned to my dressing room at the end of the day's work the notice on my door had been changed to Dame Thora Hird, all done out in beautiful letters.

Jan could hardly speak when she telephoned me that evening. Our grandchildren were both at UCLA (University of California at Los Angeles), and she immediately wanted to set wheels in motion to bring them over for the investiture. When I said the expense was to be thought about, she said – and this is typical of her – 'How many chances will they get to see their grandmother standing with the Queen of England inside Buckingham Palace – and get to be inside Buckingham Palace, too?' I gave in.

On the morning I was to go to Buckingham Palace to receive my insignia from the Queen, Jan, Daisy, James and I travelled together in the car. Scottie had forfeited his seat, because you are only allowed three people, and he said it was more important for the grandchildren, and anyway he'd been along to see me receive my OBE. So there we were. I had to go in one door, and they had to go in another one. It all takes place in the Ballroom, if you've visited Buckingham Palace, and there is a large orchestra at one end, play-ing all the time. Everything runs very smoothly and is rehearsed to the second.

I found out when I got there that I was 'first on'. Now in the theatrical world the first on the bill are called 'curtain-raisers', it's never a star act, and I said to the gentleman, 'Oh, good gracious! That doesn't sound very good. Am I to be the curtain-raiser?' and he said, 'Well, whatever a curtain-raiser is, you aren't that, because you are the only one to be made a Dame here today.'

Anyhow, then I got a little bit nervous about making my curtsey to the Queen. I wanted to do it, but having arthritis so badly I was afraid of falling. So when they pinned the little hook on my coat, which they do so she can just hang the thing on, I told them I was getting anxious, so they brought me a page to escort me the whole time, even when I did my walk up and turn to be presented to the Queen. So I managed my curtsey all right. She has four Beefeaters with her, standing ready in case you're going to attack her!

There are two pieces of insignia when you're a Dame, and when the Queen was pinning on the lower one she looked up at me and smiled so beautifully and said, 'This gives me great pleasure.' At the end, when she was leaving, Jan and James and Daisy were sitting in the front row and Daisy gave the Queen a big smile – she has a lovely smile, Daisy – and the Queen gave her a really big smile back. Daisy thought that alone was worth flying over from America for – and I'm sure it was.

Perhaps I should give Daisy the last word in this chapter. While we were having our lunch, after the investiture and before the celebration party we gave for friends in the evening, she wrote this little rhyme, which she read out at the party:

> *The papers wrote, the word was out*
> *The truth by all was seen –*
> *Dame Thora was in London*
> *And chatting to the Queen!*
>
> *She looked a real beauty*
> *Her suit and hat were blue*
> *And Jan was there, and so was James*
> *And even Daisy, too.*
>
> *At 'curtain up' she came on*
> *The Queen pinned on the treasure*
> *She smiled and said, 'Dear Thora,*
> *This is giving me great pleasure!'*

Nothing like a Dame

Dame Thora got her Dameship
Or is she called a Knight?
And then, our tummies growling,
We went to get a bite.

The Ritz was just ... too Ritzy!
So where do you think we choose?
Cheese and onion sandwiches
With Poppa, in the Mews!

And now it's back to LA –
Oh, Ganny, I'm so flustered –
You know I can't round off this rhyme
Without the words 'Egg custard'!

30

Summer Wine

In 1979 I was filming the BBC drama series *Flesh and Blood*. I was playing the eighty-four-year-old matriarch of a family cement firm.

Among all the appointments I had for it – going for shoes, going for coats and all this – I see in my diary 'Appointment with Joyce – make-up'. Joyce was a wonderful artist. She took so much pains with my wig, dressing it so carefully – because in those days I was in my sixties, playing a lady of eighty-four, and I had to wear a wig. These days I am eighty-four, often playing a lady in her sixties, and I'm happy to report – I don't need a wig!

In the latest batch of *Last of the Summer Wine*, recorded in 1995, Joyce was back with me again for the first time since *Flesh and Blood*. We were both overjoyed to see one another again. It's one of the lovely things of our business, making friends with people you work with, and then years later working together again.

I suppose Edie, the character I play in *Last of the Summer Wine*, is supposed to be in her late sixties, so I've done a complete reversal in fifteen years. Joyce said, 'They've made you up a wig, just in case you'd like to try ...' Well, I did try it on to please her, but I didn't wear it. I don't know why, but for all my complaints about my hair being too fine and too straight, it has done me one good turn by never going grey. It's still my own colour, for what colour it is, although I don't think I would have minded if it had gone pure white – I think white hair is very beautiful.

Incidentally, any minute now *Flesh and Blood* is going to be shown again on television, and I'm very interested to see my younger self playing eighty-four ... now that I actually *am* eighty-four.

The little village of Holmfirth, in the Yorkshire Dales, has become quite a tourist attraction, with posters at railway stations saying 'Visit *Summer Wine* country'. There's a pretty little tea-shop called The Wrinkled Stocking, and in the middle of the village there's a pair of stone wellingtons with a little slot at the top where you can put money in for the hospital – that's Compo's wellies. And there are many things that have come about as a result of the television series that I would say have made Holmfirth into a very thriving, prosperous little place.

Of all the people who have stopped me in the past eleven years or so to make any remark about *Last of the Summer Wine*, only one person, a lady I met on a train, has ever in any way shape or form run it down – and that was because she lived in Holmfirth, and seemed to hold me personally responsible for spoiling her peace and quiet on a Sunday! I suppose you can't blame her, really, if she'd moved there hoping to get away from it all.

Everyone else I've ever spoken to has always said how much they enjoy it, and how they only wish it was on every week. So I reckon that Compo, Clegg,

Foggy and company will go on a bit longer yet. There can't be much wrong with a series that has been so popular for twenty-five years.

I've had some good directors in television – a joy to work with, so many of them – and I've got to say about Alan Bell, who directs *Last of the Summer Wine*, that he's Dr Barnardo to me, and to us all. He never loses his temper ... he just quietly goes on. And another thing, which is a bit technical, but I'm going to say it: someone who is an editor and cutter is always a very clever man or woman. And if you get a director on a film who has been an editor and cutter before, you're always pleased because you know that they can see in advance the shape of the scene you're doing, and where it will begin and end in the final cut. So there's never any flim-flam about doing everything seventy different ways before they finally make up their mind which one they want.

When I'd been working for six months with Alan Bell on *Summer Wine*, I said to him one day, 'Excuse me asking, Alan, but were you an editor and a cutter ever?' And he said, 'Yes, for years. Why?' And I said, 'Because it shows, in your directing.' Any artist will tell you that to work for a director who has had experience as an editor and cutter is a joy.

When Alan first asked me to play a cameo role in an episode of *Last of the Summer Wine*, I was very pleased – but I can honestly say that I thought that was all I would do. Little did I think that I would still be part of the 'ensemble' eleven years later. It isn't difficult to explain how enjoyable it is. We all have so many laughs about old times, because we're all

professionals who have known one another for ever –
I mean to say, all of us are over twenty-one, and many
of us have played together in different things over the
years, going way back. Even the smaller parts are real
old pros, like Danny O'Dea playing the man with
thick glasses who bumbles about raising his hat to
lamp-posts and generally mistaking everything he
doesn't see. He usually only has one line per episode –
but he always gets a good laugh on it because he's a
wonderful comic, one of the best.

The thing people nearly always comment on to me
is the business I do with putting down newspaper
underneath my husband's anatomy wherever he
walks, stands, sits or leans. It seems to strike a chord!
To be honest, I have so few lines in each episode I'm
glad to have a bit of business that I can have some fun
with. With the newspapers, I can make it funny by
managing to shove one under his hand or his elbow or
any other part of his anatomy he's just about to put
down – without even looking at him. I enjoy that, and
the coffee scenes, when we all lift our cups at the exact
same moment. These things get a good laugh, if you
get the timing right to the split second, because they're
funny when they happen in life. That's what it's all
about, really.

It's a joy to share a caravan with two old friends,
Kathy Staff and Jane Freeman. The three of us 'run the
country' very successfully from our little dressing
room on the moor! There's a lot of laughing, a lot of
serious talk, and a lot of affection in our little caravan
... which also has a 'little' lavatory – none of us can get
into it, especially not Kathy when she's wearing her
'Nora Batty' padding!

151

I do hereby declare that if it happens to be a cold day on the edge of the Yorkshire Moors, and my arthritis is being a bit more painful than usual, the kindness of Kathy and Jane is such that, well, they couldn't be kinder, that's all ... There is kindness and there is great kindness, but their kind of great kindness is of the super-kind kind.

But, like I said, it's a comedy about old people, and none of us in it has still got our twenty-first birthday to look forward to. Next to my bed at home I have a little framed saying, the first thing I see every morning, and it says

> *'Don't stop doing things because you're growing old –*
> *you only grow old if you stop doing things.'*

I think it's so *true*. The one thing that has helped me most is the fact that I have been able to keep on working, because for me that is the thing I am most afraid of, not being able to work. I have had arthritis for a long time, and anyone who has got it knows the sort of pain that is. I always say to the Lord, 'I won't complain about any of the pain I get when I'm not working, if you take it away when I do.' And he does. As soon as I start working – whatever it is, the pain disappears. So I try very hard to keep my side of the bargain.

For a short while last Spring, though, I thought that my working days might be over. It was in April 1995, and I was down in the country where I have a cottage, and all of a sudden when I put my foot on the floor – whoohoosh! – I've never known such pain in my life.

I really have not. Fortunately Jan was there. She said, 'What's the matter?' And I said, 'I can't get up.'

She rang my doctor in London, then she packed my house up, put all the food in the car (it's a two-hour drive) and we got there for seven o'clock. The doctor examined me and said, 'This is a hospital job' I said, 'When? Tomorrow?' And he said, 'Tonight. I'm sending for the ambulance.' So I went straight to hospital.

I had had both hips replaced in 1980, and I'd had my right hip replaced a second time, which is as much as any surgeon wants to do, but this time it wasn't the hip, it was the bone from the knee to the hip, the femur, that was not holding the replacement hip as it should. So I've got a longer metal piece there now, but I can't tell.

Surgeons are brilliant people, and are always accorded a lot of respect. When they come round to your bed – and anybody reading this knows what it's like, if you've been in hospital – it's a royal visitation. Mine said, 'You see, Mrs Scott, it isn't usual for us to cure a lady of eighty-three ...' and here he paused dramatically '... to go back to work!'

I didn't like that, but I didn't say anything. And about two mornings afterwards he came round again, with another surgeon, and he asked me, had I any pain? and I said, 'Well, it's a little bit painful, but ... no, no, I'm really doing marvellously.' And he said (again), 'I should think you are! You see, we aren't used to curing people of eighty-three ...' (dramatic pause for effect) '... so that they can go back to work!' I didn't say anything, because I wouldn't be rude to this brilliant man, with the other surgeon and all the nurses fluttering round him. But the third time he

153

came round he had a set of students, and he was telling them all about what I'd had done, and then he turned to me and he said, 'You see, Mrs Scott ...'

– and I held up my hand and said, 'Don't say it! Please!'

'Say what?'

'That you are not used to curing people of eighty-three ... to go back to work!'

And he laughed, I will say. I didn't mean to be rude, but I thought, 'If he says that every time he comes round ...' Because I had every intention of going back to work, you see. It was what was keeping me going.

Acting happens to be the kind of job you can go on doing long after normal retirement age – if anyone will have you! I mean to say, plays are about people, and all people grow old, so old people can have parts.

I had my operation in April 1995, and was due to be rehearsing for the new series of *Summer Wine* in June, and I had one fear – Alan Bell is such a considerate, good man, and I thought if ever he said to me, 'Thora, could you just ...?' and I had to say to him, 'I cannot do that, Alan' I would be broken-hearted.

So I thought it was better to be very brave, and say that I didn't think that I would be able to do the next series. And it took a lot for me to say that. But when I started to say it, Alan said, 'Well, wait a minute ... I've seen all ten scripts.' I said, 'Oh yes. And supposing that there's something that you ask me to do and ...' He held up his hand, 'Hold on! You can drink a cup of coffee, can't you?' I said, 'Yes.' He said, 'Well, you've the coffee morning in all ten. Every one. You can get in the car, can't you?' I said, 'Well, just between the wheel and the seat ...' And he said, 'Yes, well, you won't have any problems with that, because we are building a false front. And the car will be on a low loader, so there's no effort getting in. There is nothing in all the ten scripts that a dog or cat couldn't do – well, if they were clever.'

Even as I'm writing this chapter, I'm just about to go off next week and film the next ten episodes, and an extra one for Christmas. They've even organised a little golf buggy to take me from place to place when I'm there, and I know that I will be given every consideration, and I can only say that I am proud and grateful to belong to such a good-hearted, talented group of people.

31

'In the mood'

As I've said many times, if I couldn't be acting I would have to be doing something – or I wouldn't be happy. And although I'm in my eighties now, that's not really that old, when you look at the Queen Mother – on the fiftieth anniversary of VE Day, for instance, standing outside Buckingham Palace, aged ninety-five, joining in all the words of the songs, did you notice? I kept thinking, 'Oh, I wish somebody would come out and give her a chair!' I know how difficult it is to stand. (That's one thing I cannot do. I could not stand in a crowd watching anything for any length of time. Even in my back kitchen in the Mews I have little stools under the table, because sometimes, if I'm drying the pots after washing up, I have to sit down to dry them.)

Watching the Queen Mother that day, I suddenly vividly remembered the year Jan was about four. I rang up Vera, her nanny, to bring her down from Morecambe to London for VE Day. Jan had a little cardboard hat on, like a Union Jack, and it had across the front of it 'Well done, boys!' She fell asleep on her nanny's knee in my dressing room, and the little hat fell forward a bit: 'Well done, boys!' I can remember that so vividly.

One of the places I love to visit, and do quite regularly, is the Royal Star and Garter home, a retirement home for 'our boys', disabled sailors, seamen and soldiers. Four of them living there fought in the First World War. One is over a hundred years old. They help make poppies for selling on Remembrance Day. I first went there when I was eighty-one, to do an interview for *Praise Be!* There was an old boy there, Jimmy, ninety-nine, a real cheeky devil. He said, 'I fancy you, you know.' I said, 'Oh, do you?' He said, 'Yes. How old are you?' I said, 'I'm eighty-one.' He said, 'Oh! Go away! Come back when you're a bit older!'

Something they all remember, because it was very popular during the war years, is the 'thé dansant', a dance held in the afternoon, where tea was served. It was regarded as a safe, respectable venue for nice young men and women to meet one another, and in particular for servicemen on leave to meet girlfriends. Many a person of my generation remembers a courtship that began at a thé dansant. So it is only fitting that Age Concern, a charity I try to support as much as I can, should hold a thé dansant every year at the Kensington Town Hall.

Lady Mountevans, a dear lady about as high as a grasshopper, always telephones me to remind me to come: 'Dearest Thora! I don't know, I really do not know what we'd do without you! Because, you see – they expect you there. You follow me, don't you? They expect you there!'

There's a procession in, the Lord Mayor of Kensington and his wife, two or three VIPs, the Metropolitan Police Commissioner, Lady Mountevans and me. And everyone cheers – 'Hurray!' You never heard such a noise in your life. All the tables are full. They've a number on their tickets, with some wonderful prizes, Thorntons chocolates, wine, that sort of thing. One year there were three bottles of champagne, better than Dom Perignon, and I said to Lady Mountevans, 'Hey, these are a bit good, aren't they?' and she said, 'Shhh! I got them out of my husband's cellar before I came out!'

There will be the police band playing 'In the Mood', and a couple of thousand old folk, who will all have brought along their bed-slippers to dance. One year, the girl sitting next to me was very – how can I describe her? – tall, good tweed suit, non-stop smoking – and it was the actual woman that *Prime Suspect* was written about – the police woman detective. While we were chatting she noticed a small old woman dancing all by herself on the dance floor – the police band playing 'In the Mood' – this is perfectly true – twirdle-der, twirdle-der – she's got the bed-slippers on, with turned-over tops and pom-poms – twirdle-de, twirdle-do – all on her own – twirdle-de, twirdle-de – white hair, ever so thin, all her little pink scalp showing through – and 'Prime Suspect' said to me, 'Oh, look at that poor old soul! I'll put my fag out and dance with her.' I said, 'Hold on! Do you know these people?' She said, 'No' and I said, 'Well, I know 'em. Have a care!' She says, 'Ah no! I can't watch her dancing on her own.' So I said, 'Go on then.' I watched. She put her fag out, went onto the floor and said to the little old lady, 'Do you want a dance, love?' But she twirdles off on her own, saying 'Gerr'off! Whey up! I'm enjoying meself!'

She was laughing all the way back, and she said, 'You were right!'

Now, I've never wished that I could be anybody else – but there are quite a few people I greatly admire. I could mention fifty, but that isn't what this book is about; so I'll just tell you about three extremely dedicated, capable women who are also my dear friends. Sandy Chalmers is Judith Chalmers' sister, and for many years was at the BBC but now works full-time for Help the Aged – and believe me, they are so lucky to have her and her colleague Pat Banon. Dorothy Crisp is the Welfare Officer at the Star and Garter Home, looking after the old boys there with great love and care; and Monica Hart works for the Stroke Association.

They work like wallop for their different charities, and what always impresses me is how clever, conscientious and reliable they are – if they say they'll do something, it's done. If I was half as good as any of them, I'd be proud of myself. So I would like to put on record, in this book, what a pleasure and an honour it has been to get to know them and to call them my friends.

32

The new girls

People are always saying to me 'You do enjoy your work, don't you?' and I do, because it brings me into contact with such a lot of nice and clever people. I could sit for hours talking about 'old pros' and the stars that people of my age know about, but one of the great advantages of television has been that I also meet and work with some of the new very clever people, like Victoria Wood and Julie Walters. I've only been in one thing with Victoria, a play she'd written herself called *Pat and Margaret*. What a clever woman she is. She does everything so well – stand-up comedy, writing and performing comic sketches, singing and acting ... we had to do all that in the old days of Variety, but not many artists who have grown up with 'the box' have such a big range.

I've been in three plays for television with Julie Walters, two by Alan Bennett. A play I did most recently with Julie was called *Wide-eyed and Legless* ... Please don't ask me why it was called that ... I do know that it is a wonderful play, based on real characters and a true story. It was also an extremely sad play – which was strange, considering the three main parts were played by Julie Walters, Jim Broadbent and myself – none of us exactly known as tragedians. Julie played a woman with that terrible illness they can't seem to get at the bottom of, ME, Jim Broadbent was her husband, and I was his mother, getting the first signs of Alzheimer's, but not so bad she has to be put away. I had some very comic lines, but everything had a sadness about it. It was beautifully written by Deric Longden, the man whose true-life story it was – the man Jim Broadbent was playing – and adapted for television by Jack Rosenthal. Deric was kind enough to say to me afterwards that I *'was'* his mother – I'd portrayed her exactly how she had been. So that was nice.

I always enjoy working with the 'new' talents like Victoria and Julie – well, they're young compared with me. They are brilliant and they are assured. Their approach to the work is different from the way I was brought up. I can see that, although I find it difficult to explain. I'm not criticising, but it is different. I am sometimes a bit surprised, I will say, how even very young artists these days – and, I mean, sometimes it's children I've acted with – will talk back to the director, and argue with him or her. I would never ever have done that when I was starting out, and it's rare for me to do it even now.

If I were to pass on any advice to a young person thinking of coming new into our business today, I would say two things are most important: first of all – be on time. My father taught me that, and it is really so important. I'll never forget the time I was in a play he was directing, and one morning I arrived for rehearsals out of breath from running and one minute late. He said, 'You're late' and I said, 'Well, only a minute ...' and he said, 'There are sixty people in this room, Thora, waiting to begin this rehearsal, and I'm here, that's sixty-one, and with you it's sixty-two. So you have wasted not one minute but sixty-two minutes of people's time. Don't be late again, and please apologise now to everyone you have kept wait-ing.' I went round the room apologising to all the actors and extras – the play was *The Desert Song*, so there were dozens of them – and I never was, and never have been late again. Early? Often. It is true, what my Dad said, that if you begin the day by keep-ing everybody waiting, it will get the whole cast, not just you, off to a bad start.

The second thing I would say is most important is to do your homework. I mean by that, don't wait until you arrive for the first read-through before you begin to study your part. Read the whole play and then your own part several times before you arrive for the first rehearsal. This, too, is out of respect for your fellow-artists. Some actors will turn up to the first read-through without even having looked at their script beforehand, and won't put any expression into their reading. I think this is depressing for everyone.

I would say that if you've got any talent, and you keep to these two rules – being on time and doing your homework – you won't go far wrong.

Well, I think that's about enough from Mrs Perfect for this chapter, don't you?

33
Monologues

In the Victorian period 'The Monologue' was the great thing, a recitation with music at the back. Even if you couldn't sing, you could always do a monologue. We had a big trunk at home, with music in, pictures of artists like Little Titch on the front, and lots of monologues – heartbreaking some of them were! I wish I still had that trunk and its contents today.

You need a pianist who can play you perhaps a dozen chords. Seven chords will go to any monologue, if the meter is da-da-da-de, da-da-da-de, da-da-da-da-da-da-de. A good pianist will put a few twiddles in as well.

When I was doing a Sunday morning job recently in Chichester Cathedral, with Don Maclean, they sent me a script – and I could not believe it. It said 'Thora recites "The Lion and Albert"'. And I said, 'But it's a religious programme!' And they said, 'Oh, well! We'd like you to do it anyway.' I'll never know why. But I loved doing it. You can tell a professional comic has written it. My favourite two lines are:

'It just goes to show', said Mother, 'that the future is never
*   revealed –*
If I'd known we were going to lose him – I'd have not had
*   his boots soled and heeled!'*

I used to perform a lot of monologues in the old days.
I even wrote one once. It's a bit risqué, but you'll
forgive me, because I was much younger then! There
was a disaster many years ago, in the 1950s, at
Lynmouth in Devon, when the River Lyn flooded and
swept away homes and everything in its path, and
many lost their lives. Morecambe, my home town,
were giving a big charity concert to raise money for
the relief fund, and they asked me if I would go back
and appear in it, because I was at that time appearing
in the West End. I said of course I would go, which I
did, early on the Sunday morning.

It wasn't until I got on the train that I thought, 'But
what am I going to do? I can't just walk on and say –
this is Thora ...'

In those days – it may be the same now, I don't
know – *The Observer*, the Sunday paper, had quite a
wide border round the edges. I had a pen, so I
thought I'd try to write myself a monologue on the
border of the paper. So I wrote it on the train, and was
able to perform it that night. It went something like
this:

Now I'll tell you a tale that will make you turn pale
It's a tale full of pathos and strife,
It's the tale of an actress who tried to get on
Well, in short, it's the tale of me life.

Monologues

Now my parents were clever – well, of course, they were
   'pros'
And the theatre was well in me blood.
My father, an actor, was top of the bill and he worked
... When he could ... If he would.

As a child my ambition had only one trend –
To appear at Dru-ary Lane
And to hear cries of 'Thora!' each night without end
And take curtains again and again.

At a quite tender age I appeared on the stage
As 'Willie' what died in East Lyn.
How was I to know that by being in that show
I'd embarked on a life steeped in sin?

Well, to panto I strayed and a big hit I made
– I used to take bow after bow –
The producer was rude and exceedingly crude
'Cos he cast me to type – as 'the Cow'!

When the pantomime's run – of a fortnight – was done
All the rounds of the Agents I went.
I was in great demand – you can quite understand –
I soon found a job – in the Big Tent!

As I entered the ring in a pink-sequinned thing
'The show must go on!' I'd repeat.
I was no common flop, for I'd got to the Top ...
I was getting twelve bob, and me keep.

I met a knife-thrower – a nice kind of chap
Who said that he'd had seven wives.

Is It Thora?

Though he'd treated 'em well, he'd a sad tale to tell –
How he'd lost them through chucking his knives.

Then one day along came the Ringmaster's son –
He was tall, he was dark ... he was **bad**
And he told me of things that I knew nowt about
And of pleasures that I'd never had.

So I met him that night by the old rustic bridge
And I knew there was something astir.
Perhaps it was fate – but I found out too late –
I was tripped, and I slipped ... What a cur!

At this time of my life I became lady wife
Of Lord Cheetham of Rogham – pronounced Dan
With his gifts and his smiles and his saloon bar whiles –
Well, he won me ... the dirty old man!

We'd a cat-and-dog life, and I knew, as his wife,
My career would soon go to the wall.
My ambition! My art! Oh! Dru-ary Lane ...
How could I give the works to them all?

So a friend of mine got me a small billiard ball
Which I ground to powder, fine, white
I could easily slip it in his cup
– 'Cos he always had Horlicks at night.

When he came home that night I could see he was tight,
'Cos he kissed me and started to wink.
'I'm not thirsty,' he said, 'I'll go straight to bed ...
Don't bother to get me a drink.'

Monologues

Then I noticed the cat lick its lips – and fall flat
So I rushed out to 'phone for the vet
When I called again later he sounded quite stunned –
She gave birth to a small snooker set!

Well I stayed on with Dan, and I'm happy to say
That now I'm at Dru-ary Lane.
It took a long time, and it's been a hard climb,
But I knew that I'd get there some day.

I take the full stage, and I'm called, like I said,
And there's no one gives back-chat to me.
I'm adored by the men ... each morn, eight to ten,
I'm the star bluddy cleaner *– that's me!*

34

'Kipyrairon'

'Kipyrairon'? No, that's not Cypriot or Greek – it's English for Keep Your Hair On! When we were kids we were always using the expression KYHO – meaning don't lose your temper. However, I don't mean it in quite the same way in this story – well, it's not worth calling a story, it's more an observation: men have a lot of natural advantages over women. I've always thought that. I'm not jealous of 'em, or anything – in fact I'm jolly grateful that I was born a female. Oh yes! They're welcome to being men as far as I'm concerned!

But just think – they don't have to bother to wear make-up; they can wear the same suit for months; they can wash their hair in two minutes, run a comb through it and immediately look smashing, sexy and sinful; they don't suffer the worry of periods, or the absence of periods; and, of course, their biggest advantage of all comes when they go to the toilet to spend a penny.

Anyone like me, who wears slacks most of the time, will be familiar with the drill: unzip slacks, slacks down, roll-on down, tights down, panties down ... and then the return journey, or second house or however you wish to describe it. I don't wish my scribblings to cause any offence ... but this is true, isn't it? A fellow just stands there, for no time at all, unzips or unbuttons, performs, zips or buttons, takes his bow and walks away, while we ladies are still only halfway through Act One, Scene One ...

Men do have one great disadvantage, though – so many of them go bald. And by 1993 Scottie had gone a bit thinner on top – well, quite a lot thinner on top, to tell the truth.

Now, I had never thought, in all the years we were married, of enquiring about where he went to be 'tidied up' or how much it cost. He told me often enough about when he was a little lad, and how his Auntie Emma used to send him to the local black-smiths for a haircut. His mother had died when he was seven years old, and in the village where he used to stay with his Auntie the blacksmith didn't only shoe the horses, he cut hair as well. Little lads like Scottie acquired his services for three ha'pence – a penny halfpenny! And I can remember my brother Neville, who had dark curly hair like a retriever dog, having his hair cut by Mr Hodgeson the barber – for threepence.

Well, by 1993 Scottie was no longer a little lad, but he had a lot less hair than when he was, so when he said one day, 'Shan't be long, love. Just going to have my hair cut,' I thought nothing of it. When he returned I couldn't see much difference, to tell the truth, but I made no remark until we were having a cuppa about half an hour later, when I said, 'He hasn't taken much off, has he?'

'No ... but it feels tidier.'

'How much does he charge, as a matter of interest?'

I asked as I started to pour him a second cup of Earl
Grey.

'Five pounds fifty.'

'!!! *How* much?' I asked, nearly dropping the teapot.

'Five pounds fifty. It was six pounds fifty where I
used to go.'

Now I was not a wife who ever grumbled about
what Scottie spent. We had one purse between us, and
one never questioned the other ... But *five pounds fifty
pence!* Just to clip off a few hairs!

A few minutes later a friend of ours, Edgar,
dropped by, and bearing in mind we knew him very
well, when I was pouring him a cup of tea I said, 'Hey,
Edgar ... how much does it cost you to have your hair
cut?' and I started laughing, not to be rude, but he's
very nearly bald. 'Six pounds fifty' he said. Honestly! I
nearly had to have a tablet. After that I kept bringing
the subject up, with all my female friends, and they'd
say things like: 'Oh ... ten pounds?' or 'I think he pays
about twelve pounds. Of course he has a manicure as
well' or 'I think it's about eight pounds, ten pounds
fifty with a singe ...' I still can't get over it – but they
never batted an eyelid! It's *me*, you see! I'm still thinking of three ha'pence at the blacksmith's, or threepence at Hodgeson's, and the days when I had a
shampoo and 'marcelle' wave with tongs – for a
shilling! I must remind myself that I'm in my eighties
now – and try to 'keep my hair on'! It would be
cheaper, wouldn't it? Five pounds fifty! They must
have been charging him a search fee!

I've gifts and cards from Jan from when she was a
little girl, and I still get lots of pleasure from looking at

them now and again. I look at sweet little floral cards that cost about threepence (old money), and you can sometimes still see the rubbed-out pencil mark of the price on the back of larger, beautiful cards, that cost about half a crown (old money), and like anyone else in my age group, I'm always thinking 'Blimey! I paid £1.80 (new money) for a card just like this yesterday!' It's not that I begrudge a penny of it, but it's very relieving to be able to say 'Would you just look how much this card costs!'

It's all part of life's rich pageant, isn't it? On a par with six spring onions in a bunch, 75p (new money). Whenever I remark on the price of spring onions, which I did when I bought some just yesterday, Jan always says sensible things like, 'But you see, Mother, it's not the six onions that cost 75p. It's all the work of cleaning and preparing them, and packing them up for sale in bags.' I suppose she's right. But I mean – did you *ever* think a large loaf of bread would cost 85p? Good gracious! A two-pound loaf used to cost fourpence halfpenny (old money) when I was a child. Oh well, Thora! KYHO!

35

Things ain't what they used to be – or are they?

When you get to my age (that means old – but I don't feel it), you hear a lot of your contemporaries saying things like, 'We-ell, things aren't as good as when I was young' and 'I don't know what the world's coming to!' I know I'm getting just as bad about thinking that many things aren't as good as they were in the old days ... artists who think nothing of turning up late for rehearsals, for instance – but we won't go into that again. And I also know that sometimes things aren't 'as good as' – they're 'a lot better than'!

A case in point was on 13 July, 1994. We were down at the cottage, and Felix, my agent, rang me up to say that a certain firm wanted me to do a fifty-second 'voice-over'. Now, for the sake of people who don't understand what a voice-over is, and I don't know why everybody should, it's a voice saying nice things about the product in an advertisement, only the owner of the voice is never seen – only heard.

I've known artists who say 'Oh no! I wouldn't ever do adverts.' I do them. I'm quite happy to earn my living doing them, providing they go with the sort of person I am. And I've never been asked to do any that wouldn't.

It is amazing, when you go for the filming, to

discover that you are not the most important person, however big a star is doing the advertisement – the *commodity* is the important bit. I remember years ago doing the advert for a Dutch soap powder. The box was designed obliquely, half in silver and half in green, and I just reached out to move it and they cried out 'No! No! Don't touch it! You might fingermark it.' And anytime I went near it, they warded me off. Eventually I was frightened of this box!

When I did *Cup a Soup*, which I did for two years on and off, they had to film me drinking it when there was steam coming off the cup ... never mind that it would scald me! I only minded because I rather like it – it's very nourishing is *Cup a Soup* ... or it is when it's not scalding hot.

Years ago – some of you may remember – I was the voice-over for *Mother's Pride* bread. I used to say: 'I'm the Mother in *Mother's Pride*, you know! They named it after me.' I became very well known for that. I was doing a Blackpool show, and when I walked on with a loaf of *Mother's Pride*, we *both* got a round of applause!

But I digress. On 13 July, 1994, Scottie and I had only just arrived at the cottage for a week's break when Felix telephoned about my doing this voice-over, so I said, 'No thanks, Felix, because we're only just down and Scottie and I want to spend some time together.' An hour later the telephone rang again, and it was Felix to say the client had been on again, offering twice the money. And I said, 'It's still "no" Felix, because I want to stay down at the cottage with Scottie.'

The following day Felix rang up again: 'How does

this grab you? They'll send a chauffeur and a car to your cottage, take you and Scottie into London, you'll do the recording, the car will wait and take you both back?' Our cottage is two hours from London, so that would be four hours' driving for a fifty-*second* voice-over. (And you're wondering about how far away I've got from 'things aren't as good as they used to be', aren't you? Go on – admit it!)

Well, I first came to London at the end of 1938 on a film contract with Ealing Studios, and by 1940 and for the next two or three years I was doing quite a few voice-overs. In those 'good old' days nearly all the filming for cinema adverts was done in underground cellars in and around Wardour Street. You would go through an ordinary street door and then down a lot of stone steps, dank and dark, into musty cellars that must have been under the London streets in Dickens' day, and looked it, and felt like it ... it was for the simple reason that the thick stone walls shut out all the sound of the London traffic and street noises, so they were the quietest places to do this sort of work. Safe from bombs, too, I imagine.

In those days, with a bit of luck, after you'd been working for an hour and a half someone might say 'Wanta cuppa, darlin'?' (You can probably imagine what an important person I was in those days – just down from Morecambe!) The tea would have been brewed about three hours before, because in wartime nobody ever threw old tea away – they just added more hot water. The only *good* thing you could say about the tea they gave you then was that it was wet ...

So that was in 'the good old days'. Now we come

back to 13 July, 1994. The chauffeur collected Jimmy and me from the cottage and drove us to London, stopping at the entrance to a little cul-de-sac, at the far end of which was a very grand main entrance, surrounded with nearly a foot of brass. Inside was a lift to take us *up* – not *down*. Just as the lift doors opened to let us out on the second floor, a smooth young gentleman stepped forward to greet us saying 'Tea ... coffee, Dame Thora? Or would you like breakfast?'

Now that's the first thing he said, I swear to you: 'Tea ... coffee, Dame Thora? Or would you like breakfast?' We went into a beautiful place, with a three-piece suite in flaming red ... I don't mean *flamin' red*, I mean flame-coloured upholstery. Every glossy magazine and newspaper were laid out on the sofa table, with plants and vases of flowers on every polished surface. A young fellow was half hidden by the flowers on the reception desk, where the telephone never stopped ringing, and he never stopped asking us if we'd like some fresh coffee. Eventually I went into the studio.

It took no more than thirty minutes to record the voice-over, and then we came out. The car was waiting to drive us back to the cottage, and all the way home I was thinking 'Why would people say things aren't as good? Things are flippin' well a *lot* better than I remember 'em!'

Another thing – when I first started in the business, because I played so many bit parts I always had to be at the studios at 6.30 in the morning for make-up, because the small parts had to be in first, so the stars could come in later. Then the Actor's

Union, Equity, made it a rule that nobody had to be in earlier than 7.15. So that's something else that's much better now.

Never mind 'It's the best thing since sliced bread' – there's been lots of better things since sliced bread. You are reading the words of someone who was here before the birth of *Zebo*. When I was a girl, before black-leading the grate, I had to mix the black stuff up in a saucer, and it was awful if you got it on your hands, because there were no rubber gloves ... rubber gloves! That's something else, you see. And now, you don't need to black lead the grate anyway, with the invention of electric fires, and central heating. You don't have to clear out the ashes first thing in the morning, going out in the icy cold in your pyjamas ...

Then there are the toiletry things you get now ... with wings. Nearly every advertisement on the box is a young woman saying 'I don't know I'm wearing one' or 'I feel so assured ...' (I'm sure you know what I'm on about.) Then there's men's aftershave, as long as they don't wear more than just a dab ... and clean men! After all these years men can come into a room and you don't know if it's a man or a woman. A man always had a leathery smell. It wasn't at all bad, actually, I didn't think, but you certainly knew they were there.

And if anyone is still not convinced by this little tale that some things *are* better now than they were then, I'll say six words to you:

'Duvets – washing machines – *Marks and Spencers*!'

36

High days and holidays

In my job I've always been able to get out of London quite a lot. For instance, on *Praise Be!* I journeyed all over Britain to interview people, and on *Last of the Summer Wine* we do the filming in Yorkshire. Every time that I'm driven along the edge of those beautiful Yorkshire moors it strikes me how lucky I am to work among such beautiful natural scenery, the miles and miles of white and purple heather.

I've been travelling to and from Yorkshire regularly over the past twenty years, because so many of the series I've been in have been made there: *Flesh and Blood*, *Hallelujah!*, *In Loving Memory*, *Last of the Summer Wine* ... as well as roles I've had in *All Creatures Great and Small*, *Heartbeat* and many others; even some of the Alan Bennett plays have been made up there. So let's put it this way, I've always had less chance than Scottie of being bored. He stayed at home seeing to everything – VAT, book-keeping, future work, cooking, shopping ... everything. He never moaned – well, hardly ever. And so it was only fair that he should be the one to choose where we should go on holiday when the diary said we could. And I'm here to tell you, Scottie became a World Expert at finding interesting places for us to visit.

When one thinks of the sad situation in the former Yugoslavia, the dreadful killings and people driven from their homes, I find it difficult to believe that in the 1970s Brian Rawlinson, the actor, who is a very dear friend of ours, and his friend Billy, and Scottie and I all went there for a holiday together, and there was more laughing in that fortnight than a lot of people have in their lives.

When Brian comes round to see me, which he often does, to this day we still talk about it. The whole holiday became like a spy romance that we all took part in, and all because Brian had just bought a beautiful white Burberry coat. When he came up to us at Gatwick, where we were all assembled because it was a package holiday Scottie had booked us on, he was wearing this new white trench-coat and a pair of dark glasses and Scottie said, 'My God! You look like James Bond!' And Brian said, 'Hush up! Tell no one. I am.'

I was reading a romantic novel by Mary Stewart, which tickled Brian because he's a bit of a clever head, and when we got to the hotel we were all trying to describe everything we saw as though in a Mary Stewart romance: 'The sunlight glinted on the fine gold hairs of his hand ... she waved at the figure on the hill with her chiffon handkerchief ...' and the holiday rapidly developed into a Mills and Boon/spy story.

We went by coach to Split, where Diocletian, or one of those Roman Emperors, had built this enormous palace – so enormous that after the Empire fell the people just filled in the spaces with houses and shops, so you actually go into Split through the gates of a palace. Of course now the town has spread all round outside the palace walls as well.

From Split we got on a boat and cruised among the Dalmatian islands, and ended up in Dubrovnik. We sailed among 'a thousand islands', I think they said, on an old British steamship, and in the dining room the columns were square with a mirror on each side, bevelled mirrors, and all the trimmings were oxidised brass. A real old British steam yacht, with tremendous atmosphere.

We started to pass notes. I gave Brian a letter 'from the War Office', saying 'You know exactly why we've sent you ...' On one of the islands we sailed past there was an old wartime defence block thing, and on it there was an upside-down anchor. I was leaning over the rails, clutching Brian's arm and saying out of the corner of my mouth – by this time we were saying nearly everything out of the corners of our mouths – 'Do you see the anchor?' as though it were a coded message!

As I turned away I looked up and saw a lady with long black hair tied back, and I hissed 'Don't turn round!' Of course Brian did turn round, and said, 'It is! It's her! It's Sonia! She *knows*.'

This woman was really from the cover of *Vogue* – rock pink trouser suit, turban to match, straight black hair tied back in a bun, and Brian said, 'Oh, she's a spy. She's Sonia, a well-known spy.' And whenever she appeared after that we'd be saying things like, 'Don't look now ... your six o'clock. She's here ...'

Scottie came out of our bedroom one morning, on the ship, and kicked over a wine bottle. He picked it up, and there was a note in the top, and I heard him laughing and he came back in and said, 'Hey, look at this.' It said, 'You will get your final instructions when

179

...' and then 'bullet holes' had been burned into it with a cigarette. And the signature started, then slid downwards ...

We went all the way up to Montenegro and the palace of King Og. The road there really climbed, hairpin bends all the way up to the high plateau. I hate heights, so I had to get down on the floor of the coach.

It's all limestone, that's why it's so beautiful, and the rock goes right down into the sea – there are no beaches in Yugoslavia, just little concrete platforms that you sit on. All the places had an atmosphere. That whole coast. We sat on the concrete beach. Every time anybody passed, Brian would look at me significantly ...

Years later, when the troubles started and they were bombing Dubrovnik, Brian rang me up and said, 'Oh, do you remember, darling, we sat under the stars there every night?'

We did. We went to a concert in the old Venetian palace. And it was there, in the garden, under the walls of the old Venetian palace, that we spent our last evening ... We were sitting outside and we had just got to the coffee and petits fours, and it went quiet and Milan, our tour guide, leant forward and said in a strange, very deliberate tone, 'The stars are very bright tonight.' It was the way he said it – very softly and deliberately ... like another coded message!

Brian leapt on the chair and said, 'It's him!' Then he pulled out a toy gun he'd bought that afternoon as a present to take home to a nephew, and went 'pank! pank! pank!' with the caps.

You wouldn't do that today in Yugoslavia ... Scottie was saying, 'You daft bugger. Get down! You'll have

us all arrested!' What was so funny was that there
were all these rather solemn ... Serbs? – I suppose they
would be, wouldn't they, in Dubrovnik? – and they
just sat there. Nobody turned round. Nobody asked
'What are they doing?' Nobody anythinged. They
didn't look up from their dinner.

When Brian got home I sent him a letter 'from the
Foreign Office', posting him to some terrible outpost
of the Empire ... And eventually he got the sack ...
Well, we had to end it somehow.

Please believe me, our holidays are usually more sane
than that. Of recent years Scottie and I, often accompanied by Jan and William, have been on several hugely
enjoyable cruises organised by SAGA. They are holidays especially designed for retired people, and suit
us down to the ground. Jan and William can always
get off and explore wherever we land at the different
ports. Scottie sometimes would go with them, and
sometimes stayed on the ship with me, but I always
stayed on board and usually wrote my diary. Here is a
diary entry from the last one we all went on together:

23 MARCH, 1993

Believe it or not, I am sitting in the middle of the
Bay of Biscay ... in a comfy chair in the aerobics
room of the *Black Prince*, cruising into Madeira!
Jan is in an aerobics class, and I've just had a
massage on my back and legs to give my poor old
arthritic joints a holiday treat. There is scarcely
any motion as the ship sails along I-i-in the-he-
Ba-ay-of-Bi-is-ca-ayo. The four of us, William,
Jan, Scottie and I are enjoying a little cruise,

calling in at most of the islands of Tenerife. The
food is splendiferous and I'm having a lovely rest.
I shall be free for a couple of days after we return
home – just enough time to unpack, chuck the
dirty laundry into the washing machine – before I
begin the next series of *Praise Be!*

As I've told you, Scottie and I moved into a cottage
next door to Jan and William's home in Sussex. This
next extract from my diary is about a 'day trip' we
made, and goes to show what a happy time can be had
without ever leaving our own shores. If you haven't
ever been to Bosham (pronounced Bossam), promise
yourself you'll go someday.

TUESDAY 5 APRIL, 1994

Last night my bloomin' old arthritis was such a
nuisance after I went to bed that by 3.45 in the
morning I had never shut my eyes. Now I have
no intention of being a moaning Minnie, but
when I got up this morning I was so tired and felt
so rotten that I could scarcely walk from one
room to another. Jan was to call round at 9.30
because Scottie and I wanted to do some shopping, and she was going to put my wheelchair in
the back of the car and drive us.
(From now on I shall refer to my wheelchair as
my WC if you don't mind – no offence.)
When Jan arrived I asked her and Scottie to
excuse me going with them. I will admit that after
they had gone I felt a bit sorry for myself, and
lonely. Silly cat. And after another cup of tea and
a look at the paper, I was thinking, 'I'll do a spot

of watering ... no, I won't, I'll clean that copper kettle and get it brighter ... no, I won't, I'll clean the front door knocker and letter box ... no, I won't ...'

By the time I had finally got my cleaning equipment out and started work on the door brasses, Jan and Scottie were back, packing items in the freezer and fridge.

Then Jan suggested I got my hat and coat on and we all drive to Bosham. Scottie suggested we lunch there. I suggested I got myself ready pronto.

The sun was shining on the sea of Chichester harbour as we drove past, and everything looked so clean and bright, with glorious boats bobbing about.

The houses at Bosham are all beautiful and the gardens cared for. The ancient church is embroidered on the Bayeux Tapestry in France, or at least a part of it is. Scottie and I had visited Normandy with Brian and Billy in 1966, and we'd seen the Bayeux tapestry. Bosham was where Harold had his fort. He had sailed from Bosham when he was captured by William of Normandy, William the Conqueror, and was made to swear that William could be the next king of the English after Edward the Confessor died – which is all shown on the tapestry. I said to Jan how peculiar it was that we should have seen the church on the tapestry in France before we ever saw it here, in our own country.

After lunch we walked – well, I didn't, I was pushed in my WC – along the sands and all

183

around Bosham. We arrived back at Jasmine Cottage in time for tea, but Jan excused herself as she wanted to take her dogs out for a walk. What a lovely, unexpected trip ... and what a daughter!

37

Jasmine Cottage

In 1993 Jan and William sold the Mill House set in its lovely grounds at Isfield. It was a hard decision, but their children have all grown up now and are away studying or working and they visit at different times, so no longer need to each have a room of their own. Jan and William decided to look for a smaller place with less land to look after. This of course meant that the cottage that Scottie and I had enjoyed staying in for eleven years was sold along with the estate. We had enjoyed every minute of our time there, so we couldn't grumble, and didn't. I was very busy, as usual, so hadn't much time to feel sad about missing our lovely country weekends. One day the furniture van arrived at our London address and neatly deposited all our cottage furniture and belongings in the garage, which, as I've described in an earlier chapter, is a big one. (But no more parties in the garage for the time being.)

Jan and Bill chose a house on the outskirts of Chichester, and Jan says she has at last found her 'dream' home. She has always wanted to live in a real period Queen Anne house, and now she does, and she is delighted. I couldn't get to see it until a few weeks after they moved in, but it is gorgeous. No, that's the wrong adjective – it's beautiful – dignified – refined. That describes it better. It's smaller than the Mill House, and the grounds are less extensive, but that was part of the reason for moving – to find somewhere smaller. But the best was yet to come! Here is the entry from my diary:

9 JULY, 1994

We've all used expressions like 'Ooh, how lovely!' 'Oh, what a surprise!' or 'Oh, I can't believe it!' haven't we? I said all that as we arrived at Jasmine Cottage for the fourth time, and saw the front garden.

Our first view of it was at Christmas 1993, when we stayed with Jan and William in their beautiful new home and discovered that the cottage next door to them was *for sale!* The owners, who were exceptionally nice people, never advertised their 1780 period cottage ... they simply told Jan and William in October that they were moving, and Jan was on the telephone to us three seconds later!

In 1993 Scottie and I had joined them for Christmas, as always, and the first thing we did was take a peek at what was to be our new cottage over the handsome flint wall.

There wasn't much of anything showing in the garden then. Our second view was on 13 January, 1994, after we had bought it. Chichester was flooded and there were little boats sailing up and down the lane outside – but neither Jan's house nor Jasmine Cottage got wet or even damp. The cottage garden was a carpet of crocus and snowdrops, and I mean *a carpet!* It was breathtaking.

28 FEBRUARY, 1994:
10.30 PM

> The big day has arrived! The furniture van is here outside our London abode and we are getting all packed into the pantechnicon for the cottage. It's the usual cantata – hot tea for the men on the team, and after that it's all go ...
> The van is now all packed up and our London garage looks a bit twelve-o'clock-lonely.

So it was a case of hey up! Jasmine Cottage, here we come, and on 1 March we moved in. It was our third visit, and the primroses and aconite had taken over, daffodils were in bud; later narcissi and tulips were pushing their way through.

I'd always hoped to be able to leave Scottie with what my mother called 'an easy going on'. I mean I'd always hoped to leave things arranged so that Scottie – or I – wouldn't be a nuisance to Jan and William, or anyone else come to that, after the dear Lord called one of us home. Now we wouldn't be 'next door' to them like in a town street – their garden and the high, flint wall separates the two houses – but I was thinking that Jan could be round at the door of Jasmine Cottage in two minutes if her Daddy was living there on his own. There would be no need for her to catch a train or drive two hours to London to see if he was all right. I know our daughter very well, she's like most daughters, extremely fond of her father – and me

– and for quite a few years I'd thought about this situation. Somehow I'd always imagined that Scottie would be the one left on his own ...

1 APRIL, 1994

My dear mother's birthday, God rest her. Our first Easter at Jasmine Cottage. I am sitting comfortably in my dear little study penning a few lines. It is Good Friday, and as I look out of the window I can see masses of primroses, tulips, daffodils, anemones, all a wonderful mass of colour. I am also trying to get my study ship-shape, so I can put my hands on anything without having to search. Most of my stuff arrived in large cardboard boxes unopened from our last cottage, and as I didn't pack them myself I'm having to unpack each one to discover what's in it.

Before lunch I spent over an hour looking at old Mothering Sunday cards, Father's Day cards, birthday cards, wedding anniversary cards from Jan and the grandchildren. I've packed them all away again carefully in yet another box, because they are too lovely to throw away and have been chosen with such loving care by our dear daughter, son-in-law and grandchildren. What a hoarder I am ...

SATURDAY 2 APRIL, 1994

After a very windy and wild night I'm sitting in the study and the sun is pouring in through the window. One of the fences has been damaged by the storm during the night, and Scottie is out there – I can see him – well wrapped up, repairing the damage with William's help.

9 JULY, 1994

And now in July, this – a blaze of colour. All along each side of the straight, forty-eight-foot long path from the front gate to the front door are beds of deep red rose bushes, dozens of them. William clipped them all to about four inches high in February, and now we are gazing open-mouthed at a sea of deep red blooms each side of the garden path. It seems like fate that the great red rose of Lancashire borders each side of our garden path, doesn't it? Along the outer walls of the garden the herbaceous borders are packed with every kind, colour and shape of bush and plants, and the walls smothered in climbing roses, clematis, and summer and winter jasmine, of course.

As I write this Jan has just popped in with a huge bunch of sweet peas. I don't mean just *sweet peas*. These are *specials!* Each stalk boasts about nine or ten blooms. And the colours! And the perfume! Oh, mate! She's also put some of their home-grown potatoes and beetroot in the kitchen.

I've just cleaned the brass Georgian door knocker, the door knob, letter box and key-hole on the very clean white front door, and while I was doing it I noticed a bush of the deepest purple lavender and some big bushes of pinks. Every time I put my nose out of doors I notice another plant. Some alyssum is pushing its way through the York stone path, but it looks so cheeky and pretty

I shan't dig it out or let 'the gardener' dig it out. Oh yes! We have a gardener now. Jan has finally persuaded Scottie to take on a lad for a few hours a week, and he looks more like a leading man than a gardener. But at eighty-seven it's time Scottie took things more easily.

As I sit here at my desk, in my little gem of a study, swanking about the house and garden, I must ask you to try and excuse me. In our three previous country cottages we have always had to prepare and make a garden ourselves – which we've loved doing – but here the garden was all ready for us, and just the size we can enjoy at our age.

The back door opens out not into a back garden, but onto a patio, so no digging for Scottie, just watering the plants in several very large earthenware urns – and there's even a tiny fountain. Yes, I know how lucky we are.

We've never wanted to be a trouble to Jan and William. She always says 'Well, you wouldn't be!' But we would be. But now we won't be – will we?

That summer's day in July, after I had written the above, Scottie and I sat together on a little bench, like a love seat, under the eaves, to drink our morning coffee and admire the front garden. Scottie said to me, 'Aren't those roses beautiful?' And I said, 'Aren't they lovely!' and he said, 'And aren't we bluddy lucky to have all this?'

It was our last summer together.

38

To be a pilgrim

In May 1994 I celebrated my eighty-third birthday on the Sea of Galilee, and what better place to be wished a 'Happy Birthday' by my darling Scottie than where Jesus must have so often celebrated his? You can't ask for better than that, can you?

We had arrived at the hotel late the night before, and as we are both early risers we were awake to sit on our balcony and watch the sunrise over the Sea of Galilee early the next morning. The boats they take you out in – 'dhows' are they called? – look just as they would have in Jesus' time, and even the boatmen were wearing New Testament costume, and you really feel that nothing but time separates you from Jesus and his first disciples.

I have started leading pilgrimages in my eighties – and it sounds so important that, but let me tell you here and now, the importance isn't so much as the love about it, and by the time you are reading this book I will have just come back from my third, God willing. It all came about because on one of my *Praise Be!* programmes a few years ago I had one of my little filmed chats – you would never have really called them 'interviews', it was always much less formal than that – with the Bishop of London, Rt Rev. David Hope, who is now Archbishop of York. I'd never met him before, and Valetta had decided to film me walking along a London street with my *A to Z* in hand, looking for the Bishop's Palace and knocking on the door of a little house to ask, and the Bishop *answering* the door himself, which – of course – is most unlikely. We only did all these things to impress you. And he did live in a little house, not a palace.

Well, I have to say this, and I'm sure many people have said it about David Hope – who's a northerner, by the way – he is such a *handsome* man! Oh dearie me! If you got a few of those American film directors over, they'd all be saying 'Well, we'll find a story about a Bishop, just so we can use you!'

We hit it off straight away, and had a lovely chat over a cup of tea that he had made himself in his little kitchen, and there too I met his chaplain, Rob Marshall. That was the beginning of a great friendship between our family and Rob Marshall, and it was with Rob that a few years later, in 1994, I headed my first pilgrimage to the Holy Land. Scottie and Jan came with me. We didn't know it at the time, but it was to be Scottie's and my last holiday together.

To say anything about that pilgrimage is never going to be good enough. It was marvellous. It was ... well, *marvellous* ... going to the places that you knew Jesus had been to. When I was first asked to *head* a pilgrimage to the Holy Land, I did say, 'I'm really not good enough to head a pilgrimage to the Holy Land. Why would you ask me?' To which they answered, with no sense at all, 'Because we think you are!' So that must have meant 'good enough'. But the thing was, I knew that I didn't really know enough about everything in the Bible to tell other people, so I was learning new things all the time as we went along, and I wasn't afraid to ask.

In the middle of the Sea of Galilee the captain turned off the boat's engines, and the sense of tranquillity you get at the moment when the boat is at rest – well, as Scottie said, it can't really be described in words. It was so still, you couldn't even hear water lapping against the side of the boat.

The only English people on the boat were Jan, Scottie and myself. Everybody else was German, and I don't speak a word of German.

We sailed across to a beach, not a sandy beach, just a gravel beach, with plants and things, and I cannot describe the tranquillity when we stopped. I wouldn't know what words to use, only to say that we had landed on the spot where the miracle of the two fishes and five loaves happened, where Jesus and his disciples fed five thousand people, a story I often read on *Praise Be!* The Minister with the German people stood up and went into the bow of the boat and read what I *knew* was the story of the loaves and the fishes. I don't know any German, but I knew that that was what he was reading.

When he'd finished reading he came and sat in the seat in front of me and turned round, put his elbow on the back of the seat and said to me in English, 'Do you believe in the Lord God?' And I said to him, just as simply, 'I'd be a very unhappy woman if I didn't.' And he stood up, started to conduct, and all the

Germans sang 'Happy birthday to you!' in perfect English. I found myself crying.

Anyhow, we set sail again, and – they are business-people, as anybody else is, over there – when we got off the boat there was a large, round, modern building, coffee coloured. As we walked over, the owner was speaking to Rob Marshall and a little boy came up and said something, and the fellow said something back and then clipped him hard over the ear. I thought, 'What a shame!', and the little lad ran off. In five minutes he was back, with the most beautiful brooch made of the tiniest conch shells you ever saw, all coloured differently, from the bottom of the lake of Galilee, and he said, "Appy Birthday to You!' I've still got it – the most wonderful present I've ever been given.

Scottie and I had been to the Holy Land once before, about ten years previously, and I had visited the cave where Jesus was born. There is a silver star set in the ground in the stable, which over the years has been enlarged, and you go through it into what is almost a little Cathedral. Any mother reading this will understand when I say the happiness was almost entire but for one thing – I wished Jan was with me. I remember there was a little nun there all the time, the first time I went, and I knelt there, saying a little prayer and thinking 'Oh! I do wish Jan was with me!'

Well, of course, when we went back there this time, Jan *was* with me. She was just as inspired as I was, and wished her children could have been with her. Not everyone believes that it really is the place where Jesus was born, because of course no one can prove it, but I think it was.

When we went through into the little Cathedral place Rob Marshall said, 'I think we'll have a hymn while we're here, and I think we'll have Thora's favourite.' So somebody just gave us a note 'Doh' and we all started 'Onward, Christian Soldiers, marching as to war ...' I'll never forget it.

Cana is not far from Nazareth. I remember thinking 'I'm glad Mary and Jesus didn't have too far to walk for the wedding.' It was about eight minutes by bus. We walked down a little alley to a tiny church, which was all stone, and as you went in there were a lot of huge water jars, like the jars you see in the pantomime of Aladdin.

In Jesus' time, at a meal or a wedding banquet the best wine was always served first ... well, it still is, isn't it? If you've guests coming for dinner, you get out your best bottle of wine, and you only get the plonk out later, when they've drunk all the good stuff. Without trying to be comical, the Miracle at Cana must have been performed while everyone could still realise it was a good wine, instead of waiting until they'd had so much they didn't know what they were drinking.

I stood in front of this church, with Scottie, and I thought 'It's so small. Mary could have stood just here, where we're standing, before they went into the church for the wedding.' At the wedding banquet Mary told Jesus, 'They've run out of wine.' And Jesus had answered, not in these words, but according to the people who know more about this than me, to the effect 'Well, what do you expect me to do about it?' And then he had said, 'Are those jars full of water?' And they said, 'Yes, they are.' And he said, 'Well, tell them to drink that.' And they did, and of course, what was poured out was the best wine anyone had ever tasted.

Needless to say, opposite the church – there is a little store selling wine! They don't try and kid you it was a drop that was in the original stone jars or anything like that, but they do give you some in a very tiny little wooden cup. And nearly everybody bought a bottle of wine as a souvenir, because it was so impressive, the church at Cana.

I'll never forget it. As I'm writing this now, this minute, I could be there. It wasn't cold, it was just a cool, stone, square entrance to a church. Jimmy and I had been married for fifty-eight years, and there in the little church we renewed our marriage vows together, and I've got a wedding certificate from Cana in Galilee to prove it!

I didn't know enough – in fact, let me be honest and say I knew very little about the Transfiguration. So before we went, because I knew we were going to the place where it might have happened, I said to Rob Marshall, 'Tell me about it, will you? Tell me like you'd tell a child at school.' And he did. I couldn't wait to go to see the place where it happened.

For the people who don't know this, and I didn't, it is up a very, very steep mountain, Mount Tabor, and Jesus and three of his disciples walked up all the way. We went in a black Mercedes taxi. I felt very guilty, going in a Mercedes, knowing that he'd trudged up all this way – well, we all did – but I could visualise Jesus with Peter, James and John plodding up this mountain. You can see for miles up there.

There is a community of Franciscan friars who live at the top, and, like in all these places, there were souvenirs for sale. I saw a little carved cross, not too big for a gold chain I have, and I thought 'I'll have that, if it's only to know I bought it here.' And I had the cross in my hand when one of the Franciscans, called Andrew, walked across to me and put both his hands round both my hands that were holding the cross, and he said, 'Thora Hird! Oh, I saw you in a lot of black-and-white films!' And I said, 'Half a mo! I wasn't in *that* many! I'm not *that* old!' We laughed, and then for half an hour Brother Andrew talked to me and it didn't matter what kind of simple things I asked him, it was as though he'd expected me to ask these things. Actually, he did most of the talking, and for once, even though I'm an actress, I was happy to let him and just listen, because he knew so much. And he said, 'Before you go, tell me, is there anything that you've thought very deeply to yourself, since coming here?' I said, 'Well, I've thought about it all very deeply, but what I'm going to say sounds a bit silly. As I put my own sandalled foot down, I've looked at the ground each time and wondered if Jesus put his sandalled foot there, where I've put mine.'

All the while we were talking he'd taken the cross out of my hand, and with his thumb was blessing it, moving his thumb to make the sign of the cross over and over again. And he said, 'Thora, if you put your foot there, you can be sure that Jesus put his foot there!'

The guide suddenly says, 'And that's where Jesus baptised so and so ...' and you look and you see and you think 'It's still the same. Everything else has altered, but that pool hasn't altered.' And when we went near to the road where he – you can easily get upset as well, if you're daft like me – where he was dragging the cross to Calvary, I really could see him, with this cross, dragging it, dragging it. I wish I could tell these things with the worthiness they deserve.

Because, of course, all of us who are Christians, it's like those of us who are Royalists – you see the Queen, don't you, and you think 'Oh! I actually was where she was standing!' And you see, I was. I was at the garden of Gethsemane ...

I can remember sitting on a form outside the Garden of Gethsemane, I suppose for not longer than ten minutes, which can seem a long time if you're on your own. Nobody passed. There was no one about but me. And I sat there and I thought of Jesus and the Garden. I always feel that that was the one place where I knew, for certain, that Christ had been there.

I led another pilgrimage early in 1995, to biblical sites in Jordan, and by the time you read this I will have been on yet another one, in early 1996. If you went a dozen times, you wouldn't have seen everything.

Now if I told you properly about Petra, one of the places we visited in Jordan, you would turn to whoever was in the room – and if there was nobody in the room you would turn to the wall – and say, 'She's exaggerating.' Because Petra is the most breathtaking place I've ever been to in my whole life. You're in the desert and you see these mountains the colour of Blackpool or Morecambe Rock – pale pink. The story – and I love to believe anything that is so beautifully told as this – goes like this:

Five thousand years ago there was a Bedouin alone, on his horse, and he was approaching these rock pink mountains and noticed that one looked as though there was a split from the top of it to the bottom. (Please read this with care, because it's difficult to describe it to you without taking you there to show you the spot.) And as he got nearer to this thin split in the mountain he realised it was just wide enough for him to go through on his horse. He went through, and to his amazement there he saw before him a city. Not a sophisticated city – you can still see the caves in the mountains where the inhabitants lived. And as he turned round to leave, he was stopped and he was told – now this is five thousand years ago, so I can't prove it, but this is what they say – he was told that if he told anybody about this place, he and his family would be hounded down and killed. So as far as we know, he didn't tell anybody ... but I don't know how anybody knows that that's what happened if he *didn't* tell anybody ... but I still think he didn't. (Are you still with me?)

Now then, we get to the Roman period, and a lot of Romans were riding about on horses, and they, too, found this place, and took it over.

But in all this time, the place hasn't altered. You still have to go to it either on horseback, which Jan did, or in a Roman chariot just like in the Hollywood film of *Ben Hur*, with horses pulling it and a man standing up in front. Well, Rob Marshall and I got in a chariot, and

I swear to you that this one was so old it was not refused by Charlton Heston – it was refused by Ramon Novarro! It was falling to bits. But we got in, and even the poor horse dragging us along was falling to bits. However, off the people on horseback went, and we went in the chariot. Rob put his foot down, and if he reads this he'll remember that I'm telling you the truth, and it went through the floor of the chariot!

Anyway, we eventually went through the opening in the mountains, and there were all the usual little boys selling snuff boxes, beads, all sorts of things. And on the right there was a large cave, and you know how the top of a cave is often very rough and uneven? Well, they'd touched up all the uneven bits with yellow, blue and red. It looked like a stage set for Aladdin. And all round the walls of this cave were necklaces and jewellery, and one thing and another – and all absolutely caked with sand and dirt. Because the fellow can't shut his shop up at night – it's just a cave.

We went in, and Rob saw a coffee pot that looked – well it looked from the Bible, it was so old – and he bought that. I saw they were building a little fire in the middle of the floor. I thought, 'Well, perhaps that's something they do, just build little fires to sit round,' so I didn't say anything, I just sat round it with them, the man who owned the shop and four other men, who all looked like brigands to me, drinking mint tea.

You know the head-dresses they wear? You've seen them, the striped head-dresses in black and white, or red and white, that they wrap round their hats and over their mouths to keep out the sand – like big tea towels. I bet you didn't know that the red-and-white ones are that colour because of the white and red roses

of York and Lancaster at the Wars of the Roses ...
Come on, be honest, you didn't know that, did you?
Our Jordanian guide told us, and he didn't know we
were from Lancashire, so it must be true ... I think.

I had already bought myself one of these – how
could I resist? – and I had bought one for Jan, and she
was very glad of it, because she had wrapped it over
her nose and mouth, for galloping along on this horse.
And as she passed the cave ... you've seen a horse rear
up? Jan's horse reared up on its hind legs just outside
the cave entrance, because of Jan stopping it suddenly,
not able to believe her eyes at the sight of me, crouch-
ing round a little fire, drinking mint tea with five brigands, thoroughly enjoying myself!

There were some rather lovely voile shawls, big
enough to use for a tablecloth for afternoon tea, and I
asked how much they were, and when he told me a
lady near by said, 'How much is that in English
money?' and he said, 'Eight pounds.' So I said, 'Oh!
Do you take English money?' He's got the full garb
on, flowing robes, tea-towel round the head, because
that's how he *lives*, behind this crack in the pink
mountains, and he looks at me with this toothless grin
and says, 'Do I take English money? How else did I go
to England eight times ... and marry a girl from Hull?'
I couldn't believe it, but it's true. So I paid him eight
pounds, and I've got my shawl to prove it.

I do so hope that you can go to the Holy Land some
day, if you haven't already, to look around and stop
and think. Part of it is no different from walking down
Oxford Street, but the parts where the gospel stories
happened seem unchanged since Jesus walked there.

happened seem unchanged since Jesus walked there. It makes the Bible come to life in such a vivid way. They say that every actor should do a season at Blackpool, and I say that every Christian should spend at least a week in the Holy Land!

39

'Just a tick, Jan!'

Early in February 1994 Jan said, 'Before all your furniture is moved out of the Mews garage and taken down to the cottage, do throw away or give away anything you've finished with and don't really need any more. I'll come up for a couple of days and help you, because knowing you, Mother, I know what it'll be – and you're nearly as bad, Father ... hoarding things.'

I am. I am a terrible hoarder. This is true. I look at a saucer that was probably part of a tea-set my husband bought me when we were courting, or one my mother left me, and all that's left is a saucer, and I think, 'Oh, well, I can't throw that away. No, I'll put a plant pot on it.' And as a result – a lot of rubbish I've got – rubbish, rubbish, that nobody else would keep!

Jan will come to London sometimes, and look at my desk. Now I must admit – my desk – I sometimes don't know whether to declare it open or set fire to it. There's fan mail, there's letters asking me to open this and open that. And she'll say, 'Have you gone through that pile?'

'No.'

'Right!' And she'll go through it, and I'll see her throwing stuff away. She'll say, 'Well, it's just stuff.

You don't want to know about somebody who are the best carpet cleaners round Bayswater. No, this is rubbish! You don't want this.'

I wish I could be like that, but I bet there's a lot of you reading this who are like me and keep stuff, don't you? I look in my drawers sometimes and I'll think, 'Oh! I'll have a real chuck out here.' And I find by the time the drawer goes back there's as much stuff in it as when I took it out, and all I've done is revive a lot of memories. But that's how I am, you see.

Well ... we started. There were many, many tea-chests, all full of stuff, such as piles of plates – none of them matching but each holding a memory. Cups, jugs, small glass dishes, etc. You know the sort of things I mean.

It was like a comedy play: As Jan put a pile of plates in a box ready for the thrift shop, I would be pleading, 'Just a tick, Jan ...' and pick up a chipped saucer – the only remaining bit of a tea service we bought before we were married. 'We can't give this away! I'll use it for a plant or something. Your Daddy bought me this before ...'

Pyoo – in a black bag it went, for the dustbin. Because Jan is a great chucker-awayer, do you see. And she'd say, 'You don't want this, do you?'

'Well, what is it?'

'Just another odd cup – you don't want it.'

'Well, let me look, if it was ...'

'Yes you *can* throw it away, Mummy' Jan would say, taking it off me again. 'You'll never use it, and you've three lovely tea-sets complete. And you won't use these ... or these ... or these' she would go on, putting more odd cups and saucers in with the plates.

'Oh! Do you remember when we bought those, Scottie? One Saturday morning when we were ...'

'Give them here' interrupted Jan, and two more coffee saucers and three mugs sailed into the thrift box.

For the next three hours the script never varied. 'You don't want these ... you'll never use that ... I *know* I bought it for you – thirty years ago – but it's no use now.'

I was using beseeching remarks like, 'I *will* use it, I'll use it for a plant ...' or 'My mother gave me that ...' or 'You made that for me when you were at school ...' It was ridiculous. Jan was quite right, and I really knew it. And even now, as I'm telling you about it, I can't even remember what half the stuff was.

When we got to the clothes department, she turned out piles of good sweaters, woollen cardigans ... dozens of things that were too small for me. Twenty shirts of Scottie's, all laundered, but too big at the neck because he'd lost so much weight...

'Oh good!' said Jan, 'These can go to the Salvation Army. They're always grateful for good clothes.' I started my usual protests, but she took no notice of me and off sailed hundreds of garments I'd enjoyed wearing – but, as she rightly pointed out, could no longer wear.

At this point Scottie suggested, 'We could do your shoe cupboard out next ...' but we decided to leave that for another day. I'll have to let you know how I get on in another book!

But do you know, when I went upstairs again to make us all a cup of coffee, I had such a feeling of satisfaction – yes, pure satisfaction. It wasn't rubbish we were getting rid of (not in my mind, anyway) but things that would be welcomed by people down on their luck. So it wasn't a case of 'Goodbye, old friends' but a case of passing on a lot of things that might benefit someone else.

Actually, Jan said something that was so true, and although it upset me a little at the time, or rather it moved me, it was so sensible that I'll finish this little chapter off with her words. She said,

'You see, we had to do this now. One day I'll be standing here on my own. Something will have happened to you and Daddy – it's going to, one day – and I shall be so dreadfully unhappy. So everything that we pass on to charity today, is going to be one less thing for me to look at and feel sad about when that day comes.'

40

'Well done, Scottie!'

In, I think it must have been March or April 1994, we went to a big concert on a Sunday night, in Drury Lane, where I was to receive a special Silver BAFTA award. As we went into Drury Lane, standing in front of the theatre there was an arc of photographers, and in their usual friendly way it was, 'Look this way, Thor!' 'Give us a grin, Thor!' and so on. Well, Scottie was with me, and my manager, Felix de Wolfe and Brenda, his wife. I turned to bring Scottie up beside me for the picture, only to notice he wasn't there ... he was flat on his face on the floor.

Everybody thought he'd tripped on the edge of the carpet, and they got him quickly on a chair, and a girl in a beautiful evening dress came up and said, 'Take no notice of this ...' meaning her dress, because Scottie's nose was bleeding ... 'I'm a nurse.' And eventually he was all right.

I collected my award, but I asked to be excused from the dinner afterwards, because I was very worried about Scottie. I wanted him to go to see the doctor the next day, but he said he felt fine and there was no need. In fact, he couldn't even remember what had happened. But now, I think I know what it was.

A few weeks later, one morning when Scottie came

home from shopping in Queensway he said, 'I'm so glad to be home. I was afraid I was going to faint for a minute while I was out.' I started to be a little anxious, then, about him going out on his own.

It's a funny thing to say to people in a book, is this. Well, not funny – I don't mean F.U.N.N.Y., I mean *strange*: I didn't know what a stroke was. At least, I knew what a stroke *was*, but what I mean to say is I wouldn't have known if I'd seen anybody having a stroke.

I was combing my hair in my room one morning – as you know, ours is quite a small Mews house – and Scottie had gone through into the bathroom to shave. And while I was combing my hair I heard a crash on the floor, like one of my big copper pans falling off the wall. And I called out, 'Is that one of the pans that's fallen off the wall?' He didn't answer, so I put my comb down and went to look in the kitchen. But there was no pan on the floor. I went into the bathroom and there was Scottie, fallen backwards into the bath, as if in a faint. His legs were over the side of the bath from the knee – do you follow what I mean? His knees and feet were over the side. And it sounds such a terrible thing to say, but it's true, I thought, 'Oh, doesn't he always have such clean shoes?' They were so polished, you know, his shoes. And at the same time I said to him, 'What is it, darling? Did you go dizzy or something?' And he didn't answer me, but he sort of put one arm out a little bit, so I got hold of it but soon realised that, from the position he was in, there was no way I could pull him out. There was no water in the bath or anything, but he had broken the tray that had all the sponges and soap, and it's a wonder it hadn't cut his neck open, but he was spared that.

I ran to the telephone. I'm blessed with good neighbours, and I called Gail, who is a dear friend, and said, 'Gail, Scottie has slipped and fallen. Is Bob there?' Because I knew her husband was a big strong fellow. And she said, 'Oh Thora, he's out, but hold on ...' and she hung up. So I went back into the bathroom, and Jimmy was still there, not saying anything. As a matter of fact he never said anything again. Ever. But at that point I wasn't to know that.

Suddenly Gail rushed in with a gentleman I'd never seen in my life before – well, nobody in the Mews had, he'd just bought a Mews house the week before, and as she'd come out of her door – she's an American – she'd called to him, 'Hey, Neighbour, we're needed. Come on!' So he'd followed her! Well, none of us could move Jimmy, and Gail said, 'I've rung for an ambulance.'

I have to give the ambulance service full marks – they were no time at all. And two ambulance men came upstairs, and one said, 'Go downstairs, Thora. We know exactly how to pick your husband up.' Gail and I went to the hospital with him.

I'm sure now that on that evening at Drury Lane, when Scottie fell down, he was having his first stroke, just a minor one. But this was a massive stroke from which he never recovered. There are more people than you'd ever realise die *in a day* in the world, with a stroke. Somebody dies every five minutes.

We always sat with him, Jan and I, in the hospital, in case he was awake, and yet I knew he wasn't awake. I don't think he ever really knew any of us were there.

No, that's not quite right. Our grand-daughter Daisy
flew over from America, and our grandson, and Daisy
was so upset because she loved him so dearly. She'd
say, 'Poppa? It's Daisy ... Squeeze my hand if you
know it's me.' And he did squeeze her hand. So
perhaps he did know a little.

After three weeks they made a hole in his stomach
and put a tube in to feed him, because he was rejecting
food all the time. Before this they had twice told us to
prepare for him dying that tea-time ... which he didn't.
I went home that Saturday tea-time, after they'd put
the tube in.

When I got home I went into my bedroom and I sat
down on the edge of my bed and I said, 'Please, God ...
Would you take Scottie, in his sleep?' Because I could
see this dear man, who had been so alive, so full of life
before his stroke, just lying there, responding to nothing. Well, that was seven o'clock. Seven hours later, at
two in the morning, the telephone rang. Jan was staying in the next room, so she answered it, and she came
in and she said, 'Mummy ... Daddy's free.'

I don't want you to think that because I asked for
him to die, God took him. I am quite convinced that
God would have taken him whether I'd said that or
not, because God knows when he wants you to go. It
just happened to coincide that it happened after I'd
said 'Please take him in his sleep.' And it's just that
I'm so grateful. I know it sounds funny to say that.

We went straight to the hospital, at two in the morning, with dear John Tudor, our minister, coming in
from the country – I don't know how he got there as
soon as we did. Scottie was on his side, just as I'd left
him that tea-time, *just* as I'd left him, and I thought

'Thank you, God.' And I mean, for a woman who loved her husband as much as I loved mine ... and I didn't cry. I looked at him, lying there so peacefully, just as though he were asleep.

We didn't have a funeral for Scottie, we had a Service of Thanksgiving taken by our dear friend John Tudor at Westminster Central Hall Chapel. We had his favourite hymn, 'Oh Happy Day', but really you should have been at our house the night before, when the organist telephoned me and said, 'Is this the right tune for "Oh Happy Day"?' He played it to me, down the telephone, and I said, 'No! No! Oh – no! Hold on. We'll sing it for you.' And there was Jan and me, each on a different telephone extension, going 'O happy day, O happy day when Jesus washed my sins away ...'

'OK, I've got that' he says, so he played it, and we carried on: 'He taught me how to watch and pray, and grow more loving every day ...' we got to about there, and he said, 'All right, I've got it now.' But the next day he said to me, 'Oh, I don't know ... I'm that nervous.' And to be honest, it didn't go quite right. Jan managed to keep going, but there seemed to be more words than tune, if you know what I mean, so some of us kept getting lost ... which was a shame, but there you are.

Everything else was great. We even had some of the jazz music that Scottie used to play when he was a drummer with the band; John Tudor gave a loving talk, then Scottie's best friend, Bill Price, and Daisy, and James, all stood up in turn and said how great Scottie had been and different things about him. There were many dear friends there – some had travelled from Scotland and Europe and even America – and I realised how loved he had been by so many people. And it sounds funny to say this, but it really was a joyous occasion, and at the end, when the coffin was leaving, it seemed just right when Jan shouted out, 'Well done, Dad!'

There were hundreds of letters of condolence, and they all said what a kind man he was. One man wrote who breeds carnations and said he had 'bredded' this beautiful carnation in maroon with a yellow edge, and could he have my permission to call it 'Thora's Scottie'? Of course I said he could. A little later on he sent me a picture of it, and then a little later after that I got whatever it is you get when a new 'breed' is accepted by the Horticultural Society. What a lovely thing to do.

The Ancient Order of Foresters, who had made Scottie and me life members, said that they had built a new summerhouse at one of their old people's homes, and wanted to call it 'James Scott's Summerhouse' and I thought – how he must have been loved.

In the spring of 1995 they were opening new Stroke Association offices in Staffordshire, and they asked me to go and open them, and I was so happy to do it. Scottie and his family spent a long time in Staffordshire when he was young, and his father was MD at the Majestic, and they were known in the Potteries.

There was a church service at which I spoke from my wheelchair, because I had only come out of hospital from having the operation on my leg two days before. They all showed me so much kindness, and they had put a big plaque on the wall, in slate, and it said, 'In memory of Jimmy Scott, husband of Dame Thora Hird.' Jan and I unveiled it, in Staffordshire, and we thought how nice it was that it should be there, where he had spent so many years of his youth.

Do you remember how I told you about the summer before, when Scottie and I were sitting outside Jasmine Cottage having a cup of coffee, and he said, 'Aren't those roses beautiful?' and I said, 'Aren't they lovely!' and he said, 'And aren't we bluddy lucky to have all this?'

The following summer John Tudor, who had just retired from being Minister of the Methodist Central Hall, Westminster, and who has been such a good and dear friend of both Scottie's and mine, and Cynthia, his wife, came down to the cottage one weekend. It was a beautiful day.

William and Jan had dug long narrow trenches all along the front of each of the forty-eight-foot rose beds, edging the path from the front door to the gate. They scattered Scottie's ashes all along each bed, and then covered them. So that's where his ashes are. It's nice they are resting there. John stood between the two beds and spoke about this wonderful man. Then he said, 'Your ashes are going here, Jimmy, because you loved these rose trees so much.' And we said prayers. Just Jan and William, and Rita, Jimmy's sister, were there, and John and Cynthia. I sat in my wheelchair. It was gloriously sunny, and now, every time I go down the path I say, 'Good Morning, luv!'

41

An easy going on

Jan has been a pillar of strength. She comes up on the train from Chichester to see me, and if I can get away for the weekend she'll drive me down to the country in Scottie's car, which is now my car. For a few days I will stay in my little cottage next door to her and William, and we'll visit some of their very dear new neighbours or invite them round for drinks at Jan and William's. We'll all have a lovely, happy time, and then Jan will drive me back to London and return to Chichester by train.

It's when she leaves our house in London to go back to Victoria Station for her train that the stupid ache starts. As she goes out of the door I'll lean out over the hay gate and watch her walk away, up the Mews. She seems to turn back into that little girl who used to walk up the Mews to school. And I can't stop crying. Aren't I daft? Or selfish ... or ungrateful ... or what? I know we shall be on the telephone in a few hours, saying 'Goodnight and God bless' so why the heck do I feel so miserable? However, it has now dawned on me that the reason I dare to feel miserable on such occasions is because I'm *selfish*. I mean that. Just plain, bluddy selfish. Let's have a show of hands on that ... I see. Just as I thought – carried unanimously!

Jan knows that I don't like being on my own. That's why I very rarely am. There's always someone dropping in. But she herself quite enjoys being on her own. I think that's the great difference between us. When Bill's away I'll telephone to say, 'Are you all right?' and she'll say, 'I'm loving it!' Jan likes to have a lot of 'space', as people say these days, but I don't think I really want there to be any space at all.

I'm not a bit fond of my own company. I wish I could be fonder of it sometimes, but no, I don't like Thora Hird very much to be on my own with. I can't think of any time when I've been on my own when I've thought, 'This is it. This is how to be.' I'm always so glad if there's somebody coming in for a coffee or something.

It isn't that I hate myself, and I can't blame Jimmy for this, but you see there has always been somebody there, all my married life. I'm so used to saying, 'Oh, I'll just put the kettle on.' Why do I need someone to tell that to? I don't know why it bothers me so much. I just don't like being on my own. And there's nothing I can add to that, only I shall perhaps underline it in this book: *I do not like being on my own!*

Scottie died just before our fifty-ninth wedding anniversary. I've been a very lucky lady to have had a happy and blissful marriage that lasted so long. I had no intention of pouring my sorrow onto anybody, particularly not onto Jan, because I knew how brave she was being for my sake. Nobody could have loved her father more than Jan loved her Daddy. I do sometimes feel depressed, but then I'll look at her, standing there, and she'll suddenly look just like a school mistress.

215

She can be quite bossy, my daughter! She'll say to me, 'Shoulders back! Come on! Shoulders back!' when I'm only walking from the dining room to the kitchen to wash up or something. 'Don't be bending down like that!' 'No, Mother. Don't use your stick like that – do it like this.' I said to her the other day, 'Oh, please, do let me do something right just for once ...' and she said, 'And don't be sorry for yourself!' So you see I can't win.

Only I do know that she loves me ... As I sit here writing this I can see her coming up the garden path, and this will be to *command* me to stop working for a few minutes and come and have a coffee. Which I shall obey with pleasure.

The strange thing about love is – it goes on. It doesn't die. It is a fact, you know, that my love for my husband has helped me over losing him. I love him no less, although he isn't actually with me, and I think of Jimmy's love for me so often. Wherever I've got to in life, wherever that may be, I wouldn't have got there without the love of my husband. He was always just that little supporting bit at my shoulder, and he still is now. I don't mean I see him – but I feel him there. I have photographs of him all round the house, where he is looking straight into camera and laughing – he had a good laugh – and it always looks as though he's laughing at me, and believe you me, he's with me *so much*. I just know he's there. I say 'Morning, Scottie!' to his photograph every day, and I always say 'Goodnight, God bless, Scottie.' And if that's my way of easing the pain a little – well, it's a very good way.

As I've already described, early in 1995, a few months after Scottie died, I went with Jan on pilgrimage to Biblical sites in Jordan. We'd arranged it long before, and Scottie should have come with us. One day we were standing at the top of Mount Nebo, where Moses stood and looked out over the Promised Land for the first time. We could see Galilee. There was a little Byzantine church which tradition says is built over Moses' tomb. It was like those very old cottages, wattle-and-daub, and inside there weren't any pews, just long forms, with leather tops. No backs. As I went in, I said to Jan, 'This is the sort of church your Daddy would have liked. He would have said, "Now this is a *real* church."' There was nothing, really, about it at all, only, I don't know, a feeling of love in it.

I sat down and – like many of us who've lost the ones we love – you sometimes can't cry until a few weeks after. I didn't with my mother. Sitting in this little church I suddenly thought, 'Oh, I'm going to cry.' I said to Jan, 'I'm going to cry' and she said, 'Well cry, Mummy,' and put her arms round my shoulders.

But, as I've told you, when I was doing the programme *Praise Be!* I got so many sad letters, and I really mean heartbreaking, and I'd read them, and cry, and Scottie would come in the room and he would say, 'Now, come on.' That's three words: now, come, on – which meant – 'We don't want any crying.' I sat on this form in this little wattle-and-daub church, and I felt the tears starting at the base of my stomach and coming up – the heartbreak I felt in my body – and just about a foot in front of me, I don't mean I saw anything, there was nothing to see, but as clearly as I'm saying this to you, I heard him say, 'Now come on.' And I stopped. I didn't cry.

Jan said to me when we got outside, 'Maybe a good cry would have done you good.' I said, 'No, your father told me not to.'

This book should be coming out in about June 1996, and I'll just have had my eighty-fifth birthday – DV! Because I hope I don't have to tell you – I'm not ready to go just yet! I still love life, and love my work, and as long as I can go on working and giving people a bit of pleasure either by acting or, if the day comes when I'm not asked to play any more parts, by writing, then that's what I shall be doing. My prayer is the same as the one written on the tomb of Winifred Holtby, the Christian novelist who died in 1935:

> *God give me work till my life shall end –*
> *And life till my work is done.*

Amen to that, say I.

Meanwhile, now I've finished this book and am about to send it off to my publishers, I'm off on a Christmas cruise with my daughter, and in the Spring we'll be off again together, leading another pilgrimage to the Holy Land, along with Rob Marshall. And, do you know, there's still as much acting work as ever in the pipeline? Never a dull moment, eh?

I have so often been asked by journalists who are interviewing me for newspaper or magazine articles, 'Would you have rather been where you are now when you were young, or how you were then – now?' Well, I'll tell you what I tell them. If my life was to start all over again, *I wouldn't alter a thing*.